T0311337

WORLD PREHISTORY

THE BASICS

World Prehistory: The Basics tells the compelling story of human prehistory, from our African origins to the spectacular pre-industrial civilizations and cities of the more recent past.

Written in a non-technical style by two archaeologists and experienced writers about the past, the story begins with human origins in Africa some 6 million years ago and the spread of our remote ancestors across the Old World. Then we return to Africa and describe the emergence of *Homo sapiens* (modern humans) over 300,000 years ago, then, much later, their permanent settlement of Europe, Eurasia, Asia, and the Americas. From hunters and foragers, we turn to the origins of farming and animal domestication in different parts of the world after about 11,000 years ago and show how these new economies changed human existence dramatically. Five chapters tell the stories of the great pre-industrial civilizations that emerged after 5000 years before present in the Old World and the Americas, their strengths, volatility, and weaknesses. These chapters describe powerful rulers and their ideologies, also the lives of non-elites. The narratives chronicle the rise and fall of civilizations, and the devastating effects of long droughts on many of them. The closing chapter poses a question: Why is world prehistory important in the modern world? What does it tell us about ourselves?

Providing a simple, but entertaining and stimulating, account of the prehistoric past from human origins to today from a global perspective, *World Prehistory: The Basics* is the ideal guide to the story of our early human past and its relevance to the modern world.

Brian M. Fagan is one of the world's leading archaeological writers and an internationally recognized authority on world prehistory. He is Distinguished Emeritus Professor of Anthropology at the University of California, Santa Barbara and author of numerous general books on archaeology.

Nadia Durrani is a Cambridge University-trained archaeologist and writer, with a PhD from University College London in Arabian archaeology. She is the editor and founder of *Past Worlds* magazine, and has authored and edited many articles and books on archaeology from every corner of the world.

THE BASICS SERIES

The Basics is a highly successful series of accessible guidebooks which provide an overview of the fundamental principles of a subject area in a jargon-free and undaunting format.

Intended for students approaching a subject for the first time, the books both introduce the essentials of a subject and provide an ideal springboard for further study. With over 50 titles spanning subjects from artificial intelligence (AI) to women's studies, *The Basics* are an ideal starting point for students seeking to understand a subject area.

Each text comes with recommendations for further study and gradually introduces the complexities and nuances within a subject.

WORLD PREHISTORY

THE BASICS

Brian M. Fagan and Nadia Durrani

Routledge
Taylor & Francis Group

LONDON AND NEW YORK

First published 2022
by Routledge
2 Park Square, Milton Park, Abingdon, Oxon OX14 4RN

and by Routledge
605 Third Avenue, New York, NY 10158

Routledge is an imprint of the Taylor & Francis Group, an informa business

British Library Cataloguing-in-Publication Data
A catalogue record for this book is available from the British Library

Library of Congress Cataloging-in-Publication Data
A catalog record for this book has been requested

ISBN: 978-1-032-01129-5 (hbk)
ISBN: 978-1-032-01112-7 (pbk)
ISBN: 978-1-003-17732-6 (ebk)

DOI: 10.4324/9781003177326

Typeset in Bembo
by Apex CoVantage, LLC

CONTENTS

PREFACE

This book is a narrative account of the human past, from our origins to the pre-industrial civilizations. It's not a stirring adventure story of golden pharaohs, pyramids, and lost continents. That's the archaeology of fiction and romance. The story we tell in these pages is written as an overarching narrative without any specialized emphases. We try and answer a basic question: what does today's archaeology tell us about what actually happened over the long time-span of the human experience? It's a history of humankind written not from written records, although we make limited use of them, but from the fascinating archive compiled by archaeologists. We are, after all, the only people who study the entire span of human history from the beginning to today. This is a global book, reflecting our rapidly changing perspectives on human diversity—how we are different and similar.

This is a volume for beginners, who know little or nothing of archaeology. We use as little technical jargon as possible. Nor do we dwell on the numerous controversies that surround human prehistory. We mention some of them, like, for example, those over the first settlement of the Americas, but only in passing. Our intent here is to tell you what happened more than the intricacies of why. A Further Reading section at the end of each chapters provides a brief guide to more detailed publications that cover the intricacies of the past in much more detail.

Welcome to the absorbing world of archaeology and archaeologists!

Brian Fagan and Nadia Durrani

AUTHORS' NOTE

We use the following conventions in this book:

DATES

We express dates before 12,000 years ago in years before present.
Ma – Million years ago
BCE/CE—We use BCE (Before the Common Era/Common Era)
    rather than BC/AD in this book.
"Present" for the purposes of this book is 1950 CE, the common
    usage.
All radiocarbon dates are statistical approximations. Unless stated to
    the contrary, they have been calibrated to actual time.

MEASUREMENTS

All measurements are given in metric units, as these are now the
    common scientific convention.

BEGINNINGS (C. 6 TO 2 MA)

About 3.7 million years ago, a volcano named Sadiman in Tanzania, East Africa, erupted with a cloud of fine ash. The cascading volcanic dust fell in a thin layer on the surrounding landscape at Laetoli. Then light rain fell, creating a soft, cement-like pathway in a seasonal river that led to nearby waterholes. Dozens of now-extinct animals walked along the riverbed soon afterward—elephants, saber-toothed tigers, and antelope. Another subsequent eruption sealed the hardened surface with its footprints, which included those of two human ancestors. Trailing behind them, often stepping directly into the adult footprints, are those of a child.

We have but an indirect sketch of the walkers. The imprints came from individuals between 1.4 and 1.49 meters tall. They walked with a rolling, slow-moving gait, their hips swiveling with each step, very different from the free-standing gait of modern humans. Their footprints display well developed arches, with heel and toe prints that could only have been made by someone walking on two feet—very different from those of upright chimpanzees.

The Laetoli footprints provide a glimpse of early hominins and, their discovery in the 1970s, led to the bombshell realization that bipedalism (walking on two feet) preceded growth in brain size, and not the other way round. Researchers realized that upright walking

DOI: 10.4324/9781003177326-1

Figure 1.1 A replica of two australopithecines leaving footprints in lava, 3.7 Ma.

Martin Shields/Alamy Stock Photo

meant our hands were now free. This meant we could make things— and creativity is a key attribute of our human family.

HOMINIDAE AND HOMININI

First, some genealogy. We humans are members of the order Primates, which includes two suborders, one of which includes the Anthropoids, which incorporates apes, people, and monkeys. Further up the genealogical pyramid, we belong to the superfamily Hominoidea, which also includes gibbons, gorillas, chimpanzees, and the bonobo. Within the hominoid superfamily, there's a division between Hominidae, which includes African and Asian apes, as well as us. We belong to the Hominini (or hominin) tribe, which includes modern humans, earlier human subspecies, and their direct ancestors.

To date, researchers have identified over 20 hominin species, but only some of them are our ancestors, many becoming extinct without giving rise to new species. At any given time over much of the past six million years, several hominin species co-existed. (A species is typically defined as a group of organisms that can provide fertile offspring.) It was only after around 30,000 years ago, that the other human species became extinct and only we—*Homo sapiens*—remained. But, given the scanty archaeological record for the early period, how do we know when hominins separated from non-human primates?

IN THE BEGINNING

By 14 Ma, Africa's climate was much drier than in earlier times. Hard-fruit and grass-eating hominoids flourished throughout East Africa between 8 and 5 Ma. They spent much time on the ground but walked on four feet. Unfortunately, we know almost nothing about these hominoids. They lived at a time of major environmental changes, including cooler temperatures and more open, as opposed to wooded, terrain. Today's humans are the descendants of these generalized common hominoid ancestors. As forests retreated and tropical Africa's climate became drier, they adapted to much more open savanna environments.

This was when early hominins became bipedal, perhaps because they spent more time feeding off foods on the ground. Bipedalism meant that walking assumed great importance for foraging over wider areas.

In adapting to drier environments, early hominin populations with their bipedalism could cover longer distances and had improved endurance. Apes, which were adapted to forested environments, stayed in the trees. In contrast, bipedal hominins, who potentially evolved around 6 Ma, expanded the range of territory where they obtained food. They broadened their diets, now including more meat.

The long-term solutions to living in the savanna meant exploiting patchy and widely distributed foods, while depending on reliable, and often hard-to-find, water supplies. The hominins were constantly on the move, with meat now playing a more important role during seasons when plant foods were scarce.

Most experts believe that East Africa was the main center of early human evolution. It is here that the greatest number of early hominins have come to light. But future fossil discoveries may complicate this scenario. The now-desert environments of Ethiopia and northern Kenya were open savanna grassland and woodland that teemed with herds of antelope and other mammals. These were prey for lions, leopards, and other predators, and also for our early hominin ancestors. We know almost nothing of these hominins, except the little known, probably bipedal, *Orrronin tugenensis*, who lived about 6.5 to 5.6 Ma. There is also *Sahelanthropus tchadensis*, of Central African origin. The latter may date to 7–6 Ma, which would place it at around the time of the likely divergence of the hominin lineage with that of the chimpanzee.

The date of this split depends less on the spartan fossil evidence, and more on genetic analysis of modern humans and modern chimps. By recording the amount by which the genes of the two species have diverged, geneticists theorize the time of our split. This method of timing, known as the "molecular clock", is based on a number of assumptions, which are constantly refined. And while there is disagreement over the precise date of our split, most geneticists currently put it somewhere between 8 and 6 Ma. As to the hominins that lived at the dawn of our story, certainly the two species referred to above were potentially bipedal (a defining characteristic of the hominin) yet they were also tree climbers.

ARDIPITHECUS RAMIDUS (4.5 MA)

As the centuries turned into millennia, other hominin species undoubtedly came and went, such as *Ardipithecus kadabba* of Ethiopia (5.8–5.2 Ma) (Figure 1.2). But around 4.5 Ma, a new player appeared on the evolutionary stage with the appearance of *Ardipithecus ramidus*, a small creature with a brain that was about 20 percent the size of that of a modern human. *Ardipithecus* is the best known of all the early hominins and comes from excavations at Aramis and Goma in Ethiopia. It had a skull closer to that of apes, and a prognathous (jutting out) face. These hominins were bipedal, but apparently lived in more wooded terrain than many of their successors. Various australopithecines followed, such as *Australopithecus anamensis* (4.2–3.9 Ma) who, like Ardi, could probably walk upright

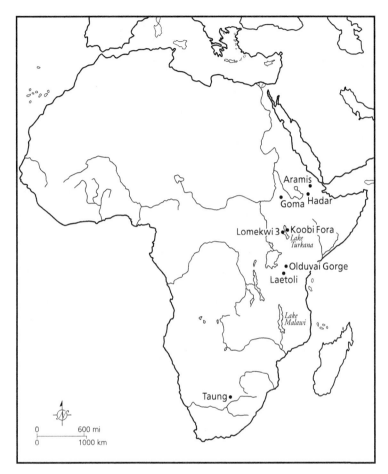

Figure 1.2 Map showing early sites in Africa.

and climb trees, possessing (once again) a combination of characteristics found both in modern apes and present-day humans.

Ardipithecus ramidus was not the only hominin in East Africa at the time. Most likely, they were the base grade from which later hominins evolved. But the exact relationship between *Ardipithecus* and later human ancestors is still a mystery.

AUSTRALOPITHECUS AFARENSIS: THE "SOUTHERN APE FROM AFAR" (C. 3.9 TO 2.9 MA)

After hundreds of thousands of years—and we're talking about long timescales here—one of the best known australopithecines emerged; *Australopithecus afarensis.* It may be the ancestor of the genus *Homo,* to which modern humans—us—belong.

Australopithecus afarensis has already appeared in this story, thanks to its footprints at Laetoli in Tanzania. These hominins are best known from the Hadar region of Ethiopia, famous for Maurice Taieb and Donald Johanson's discovery of a 3.18-million-year-old incomplete skeleton that they named Lucy. (They were playing the Beatles' song, *Lucy in the Sky with Diamonds* when they celebrated their discovery.) She was only 1.0 to 1.2 meters tall and between 19 and 21 years old.

Subsequent finds have filled in the picture. There was a marked difference between males and much smaller females. But all were powerful, heavily muscled, and fully bipedal. A 3.2 Ma foot found near Lucy's find-spot had arches, showing that *Ardipithecus* was a nimble walker. But despite this walking ability, their robust, curved arms and fingers are those of habitual tree climbers. Their brain capacity was just larger than the maximum brain size of modern chimpanzees.

At first, *Australopithecus afarensis* appeared to be confined to East Africa, but they probably flourished over a much wider area, into southern Africa. Whether or not these discoveries represent more than one species of australopithecine remains unknown, but *Australopithecus afarensis* may have been the most widespread.

Around 3 Ma, the record includes a species identified by the famed anatomist Raymond Dart in the 1920s. He recognized a small, graceful australopithecine from Taung in South Africa, which he named *Australopithecus africanus* (3.3–2.1 Ma). This was a nimble hominin, who could walk upright—despite its small brain size (samples range from 428–625 cubic cm). Dart's close ally, Robert Broom, then discovered another species, *Australopithecus robustus* (since renamed *Paranthropus robustus*), a heavy-set hominin that flourished between about 2 and 1 Ma. They had similar sized brains (530 cubic cm) and massive back teeth, which were ideal for chewing coarse, fibrous plant foods.

Due to these two species, Raymond Dart emphasized a robust and gracile subdivision among the early humans, which is still convenient. But, inevitably, later discoveries have revealed a greater diversity of australopithecines and paranthropines, especially between 3.3 and 2 Ma. This long period of time witnessed major changes in the skull and face, and perhaps more modern behavioral changes too, as our ancestors began routinely walking upright. This meant their hands were now freed up (which in turn allowed them to make things, arguably with more ease than a four-footed creature). Indeed, a site in Kenya has yielded the oldest known human-made stone tools in the world—at 3.3 Ma, which were clearly the work of one of these early hominin forms.

ENTER *HOMO HABILIS* (C. 2.5 MA)

Sometime around 2.5 Ma, we find evidence for *Homo habilis*, the first member of the genus *Homo*—to which we modern humans belong. They had larger brains, smaller jaws and teeth, also longer legs, shorter arms, and nimble hands. Their larger, opposable thumbs, like ours, allowed them to pinch and manipulate objects in different directions. Body size tended to increase. The size differences between males and females (sexual dimorphism) became less marked. These changes roughly coincided with the first appearance of stone tools.

Louis and Mary Leakey were the first to identify this earliest *Homo* at Olduvai Gorge (now often called Oldupai) in Tanzania. They named their find *Homo habilis*, "handy person", assuming that this was the first toolmaking human. Subsequently, fossil remains of *Homo habilis* have come from Kenya, Ethiopia, and South Africa, dating to between 2.4 and 1.6 Ma.

The term *Homo habilis* almost certainly encompasses several early human species, sometimes referred to generically as early *Homo*. If you had encountered *Homo habilis* about 2 million years ago, you would have seen little to distinguish the new hominin from *Australopithecus*. Both were of similar height and weight, about 1.3 meters tall and weighing about 40 kilograms. They were both bipedal, but *habilis* looked less ape-like around the face and skull. The head was higher and rounder, the brain capacity as high as 700 cc, the face less protruding, and the jaw smaller. (Adult chimpanzees have brain capacities around 384 cc.) Microscopic studies of their teeth show that both *Australopithecus* and *Homo habilis* were predominantly fruit eaters.

Homo habilis skeletons are a mosaic of primitive and more advanced features. Their owners spent a lot of time walking upright, but they were completely at ease in trees. We know this from a *Homo habilis* skeleton at Olduvai, where, like much earlier Lucy, the upper limb bones are up to 95 percent of the length of the thigh. Chimpanzees have almost equal dimensions for upper arm and leg bones, whereas modern human upper arms are only 70 percent of the length of their upper leg bones. Almost certainly, all forms of *Homo habilis* were expert tree climbers. They may have been more ape-like in their behavior than one might be tempted to believe. Indeed, it was their association with "the first stone tools" (a profound invention among the ancestors) that led evolutionists to place this species in our genus. But with the recent discovery of even older (3.3 Ma) stone tools in Kenya, the link between *Homo* and the ability to make stone tools has been broken. As a result, the status of *Homo habilis* as a member of the genus *Homo* is being questioned by some.

ADAPTIVE RADIATION

As you can see, the picture is complex. Many of our basic assumptions have been thoroughly smashed by new discoveries. Until surprisingly recently, for instance, everyone assumed that human evolution was ladder-like, with an ape-like ancestor at the base and modern humans at the top, with toolmaking as the most defining human characteristic. We now know that identifying the earliest human, let alone some unbroken ancestry over time, is virtually impossible. There were many more hominin species thriving at the time and the links between individual species are typically far from clear. Instead, paleoanthropologists Bernard Wood and Mark Collard used an intricate statistical analysis using body size, shape, locomotion, and other features to divide humans into two broad groups. These adapted to the environment in different ways:

Australopithecines and *Homo habilis* (*c.* 4.2–1.6 Ma). This group relied on both bipedal walking on the ground and expert climbing. Their body mass was low, their shape better adapted to relatively wooded environments. Their teeth and jaws, closer to those of apes, enabled chewing and biting a varied and mechanically demanding diet.

Later humans, including *Homo erectus and other species* (1.9 Ma-present) offered a significant contrast. Their body masses were larger, and their physique was adaptive to more open terrain. They spent their lives on two feet and had but limited tree-climbing abilities. Their teeth and jaws had the same mechanical properties as modern humans.

Hominin evolution resulted from a series of adaptive radiations that unfolded over about 6 million years. The first radiation was that of bipedal apes in the drier parts of Africa. Then, subsequent radiations gave rise to various hominins, each with their own adaptive solutions. Later humans radiated not so much anatomically as ecologically, spreading from Africa, and creating distinct geographic populations. In doing this, we were no different from other animals, which began as a slim stem and radiated into distinct branches.

The Wood/Collard classification creates a significant chasm between the hominins of earlier than about 1.9 Ma and those who evolved after that date. What caused this major adaptive shift in human evolution is unknown. Did it correspond with major climatic and environmental swings or was it the result of changes in hominin culture? These are fundamental questions for future generations of research.

SCAVENGING AND OPPORTUNISM

Studying the earliest humans and how they lived requires slow-moving, fine-grained research both in the field and in the laboratory. Poor preservation conditions make it hard to reconstruct the lifeways of more than two million years ago. Much of the story comes from clusters of stone tools, and surviving food remains, especially broken animal bones. A newly promising approach calls on stable carbon isotopes in bones and teeth, which gives an idea of the relative importance of tropical grasses as opposed to shrub and tree foods in hominin diets.

For hundreds of thousands of years, hunters and foragers used central places, where they returned to sleep, make tools, cook food, and engage in social activities. But did the earliest humans use such locations? Scatters of animal bone fragments, also stone tools and waste flakes have been excavated at Olduvai Gorge, also near the eastern shores of Lake Turkana in northern Kenya. One dry streambed at Koobi Fora near the lake yielded the bones of a hippopotamus, which a group of hominins came across about 1.8 Ma. They gathered around the dead animal and removed meat and bones from it with stone flakes. The butchers imported stone from 14 kilometers away to strike off flakes to dismember the carcass. We don't know whether they simply scavenged meat from the dead beast or whether they hunted it themselves.

Another Koobi Fora site named FxJj50 lies in an ancient watercourse, where one could take shelter from the blazing sun. Over two thousand bones from at least 20 animals, mainly antelope, lay among choppers, sharp-edged flakes, and battered cobbles. The visitors smashed bones and cut off flesh, for the cutting marks are clearly visible. But the game may have been killed by predators, who chewed off the articular ends of the bones. Perhaps the lions and other beasts that killed the animals fled when the hominins arrived.

At Olduvai Gorge, Mary Leakey recorded what she called "living floors", one of which yielded more than 4,000 tools and broken bones over an area 4.5 meters across. An early location in the Gorge known as Ewass Oldupa has yielded stone tools some 2 million years old. But did the hominins camp there? More recent research has shown that some of the weathered bones had lain on the surface for perhaps as long as ten years. Olduvai was, and still is, a predator-rich environment, where it would have been dangerous for hominins to remain at one location for any period of time. Many of the Olduvai bones bear traces of predator teeth as well as human activity, as if the hominins moved in and seized meat from predator kills when the opportunity arose.

We know that hominins visited the same places occasionally over periods as long as 200,000 years, using different habitats and adapting to numerous environmental changes without changing their technology. This is one of the earliest examples of people adapting their behavior to major ecological transformations. Yet they continued to use the same simple stone tools without significant modification for two hundred millennia. It was changing human behavior, not technology, that allowed *Homo habilis* to exploit a wide range of habitats effortlessly.

Opportunism has always been an important human quality and may well have come into play when our forebears spent more time in open landscapes. There, they competed successfully with other carnivores by obtaining and eating meat. The dangers of competing with other predators were outweighed by the advantages, especially more readily available, easily carried food supplies. More often than we realize, too, hominins may have been prey rather than predators. Being hunted brought evolutionary pressures to bear on our ancestors. With time, our otherwise defenseless, naked ape, ground living ancestors, learned how to use their newly freed-up hands to make things to aid their survival. These "things" included stone tools, and presumably other long-perished objects. With such creativity, so brain size began to grow, which may have been further enhanced by a new diet that began to include calorie-rich animal flesh.

Scavenging came first, yet it was never easy for relatively slow-moving animals like hominins. Success depended on close observation—of vultures gathering above fresh predator kills, of telltale antelope fur tufts at the foot of trees where leopards stashed their kills. The open savanna was an ideal and vacant niche for humans armed with simple weapons and tools. These made possible new ways of getting food and processing it, not only meat, but also plant foods of many kinds.

The minute wear patterns of hominin teeth tell us that both *Australopithecus* and *Homo habilis* thrived on a diet very similar to that of chimpanzees. *Homo habilis* and some of the australopithecines certainly engaged in scavenging. This must have involved some cooperation and advance planning, perhaps division of labor between young and old, or men and women. Some groups carried toolmaking stone over 10 kilometers from its source, probably far from the carcasses they sought. Scavenging may have begun as a way of supplementing plant foods in more open landscapes and a drier world. There's one certainty: How *Homo habilis* behaved was completely differently from pre-hominin apes, chimpanzees or, for that matter, from modern hunter-gatherers.

THE EARLIEST TECHNOLOGY (3.3 TO 1.5 MA)

We humans manufacture tools habitually and with far more complexity than other animals like chimpanzees. One reason is that our big brains allow us to plan our actions far further in advance. The sequence of moving flakes from a stone lump to produce a finished tool required selecting the correct rock. Then the toolmaker had to visualize the three-dimensional steps needed to flake it and make a tool. Finally, and most important of all, one had to be capable of passing on this knowledge to others, presumably by example.

The earliest known stone tools date to 3.3 Ma, known from the Lomekwi 3 site in West Turkana, northern Kenya. But the earliest well-studied technology, known as the Oldowan Industry (after Olduvai Gorge), dates to between 2.67 and 1.5 Ma.

Most Oldowan tools were choppers and flakes, the latter used to cut meat and perhaps wood. *Homo habilis* developed a simple, highly effective technology that became more complex over time. Eventually, the toolmakers flaked the choppers on both sides, to make simple bifacial tools. The choppers and flakes were simple, but those who made them had a skilled appreciation of basic stone-flaking techniques (Figure 1.3).

Thanks to years of research with Oldowan toolmaking, we know that *Homo habilis* could readily produce dozens of sharp-edged flakes. These studies included examining traces of edge wear, also controlled experiments such as skinning and butchering animals with replica flakes. But the hominins did not make the kinds of standardized tools made by later humans. Their tools were mainly used to process animal carcasses—skinning, cutting joints and meat, and breaking open bones for marrow. The earliest toolmaking expertise

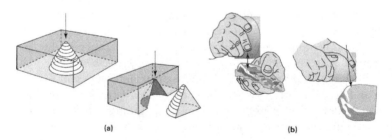

Figure 1.3 Early stone technology. Certain types of flint rock will fracture in distinctive ways, familiar to early humans. (a) The first toolmakers used a heavy hammer stone to split rocks and remove edge flakes. Or they struck edges from lava lumps to form jagged working edges. Modern experiments have shown these were remarkably effective for dismembering and butchering game animals. (b) Using a hammerstone to trim stone, and an anvil to do the same.

was opportunistic and changed gradually as humans became more dependent on technology over the millennia.

How, then, did *Homo habilis* interact with the natural world? There was a dramatic rise in meat consumption abut 2 Ma, but, in practice, all species of *Homo habilis* were behaviorally flexible, non-specialized foragers. Theirs was a diverse lifeway marked by shifts between simple hunting and scavenging, between food sharing and feeding on the move. We know that they carried cores and flakes over considerable distances, a sign that they also moved meat and other foods to different, ever-changing locations. This hints at a more sophisticated interaction with the environment than chimpanzees, who carry "tools" (mainly chewed sticks for extracting bugs from trees and anthills) only to fixed locations.

The anthropologist Robin Dunbar has estimated that australopithecines lived in groups of about 67 individuals. He hypothesizes that *Homo habilis* flourished in larger groups of about 81 individuals. Group living was essential for ground dwelling hominins living in environments like the African savanna, which teemed with predators. They had only the simplest of weapons for protection and no fire. With time, the increasingly large brain of the *Homo* genus allowed for greater social intelligence for coping with the complexities of living in closer juxtaposition to others. This would have helped survival in environments where food was distributed irregularly over wide areas. Intelligence, knowledge about the surrounding landscape, and territory beyond the horizon—and other groups—provided insurance for survival. But this intelligence would have been impossible to share fully without speech and fluent language, which developed much later.

LANGUAGE AND COOPERATION

Cooperation, the ability to get together to solve problems of feeding oneself and to deal with potential conflict, has always been a vital quality for human beings. But at what did point did hominins acquire language and speech?

Our closest living relatives, the chimpanzees, communicate with gestures and voice sounds. But they lack the vocal apparatus to talk. Unlike chimpanzees and other apes, humans acquire words and the ability to form sentences early in life. In human verbal communication, there's an important distinction between language with its mental processes, and speech, the externalization of same. Both skills were vital to human evolution because they opened up unlimited potential both for cooperative behavior and for enriching life. But when did we abandon grunts for a form of talking?

Some clues come from the brain cells of australopithecines and early humans. The brain cell of a *Homo habilis* from Koobi Fora is 300 cc larger and has a more humanlike configuration, especially in Broca's area where speech control is located.

The position of the larynx, the voice box, is high in the neck in most mammals, including humans. But between 18 months and 2 years old, a human child's larynx descends from high in the neck to between the fourth and seventh neck vertebrae. This completely alters the way in children speak and breathe. Fortunately, modern humans with a lower larynx have a distinctive arched skull base, unlike that of australopithecines and *Homo habilis.* It was only about 300,000 years ago that the base of the human skull assumed its modern curvature, as if fully articulate speech finally evolved then.

Most likely, language evolved as a way of exchanging social information within increasingly large and more complex groups. The earliest humans had more ways to communicate than merely the gestures and grunts of non-human primates. But fully articulate speech and language were a more recent stimulus to biological and cultural evolution.

The first phase of human evolution involved shifts in the basic patterns of obtaining food and moving around, as well as new behaviors—food sharing and toolmaking. Enhanced communication, information exchange, and economic and social insights followed, as well as such human qualities as cunning and restraint. With time, hominin anatomy was augmented with tools. Culture became an inseparable part of humanity as social life acquired a new, and as yet little understood, complexity.

What was it that made members of the genus *Homo* more complex? The answer is surely that we, certainly from the time of *Homo erectus* (1.9 Ma) (see Chapter 2), required greater intelligence for far more complex interactions with other people. Such increased complexity must have been a powerful force in the evolution of the human brain. Likewise, the adoption of a wider diet with a food-sharing social group placed more acute demands on the ability to cope with the complex unpredictable. The brilliant achievements of later humanity may well be a consequence of the fact that our early ancestors had to become more and more socially adept.

For around a million years, *Homo habilis* flourished over large areas of savanna and more open terrain in tropical Africa. Their stone choppers and flakes have come to light not only in Northeast and East Africa, but also in South Africa, and in northeastern Algeria far to the north. They were mobile hominins, constantly on the move, living in loosely knit bands, engaged in scavenging, foraging for plants, and perhaps running down prey such as small antelope. Their significantly enlarged brains gave them the ability to adapt constantly to ever-changing climatic changes and other events—to droughts, floods, and to earthquakes and volcanic eruptions. Unlike other apes, they thrived on the ground, cooperated and planned ahead, and adapted effortlessly to changes in their environment.

★ ★ ★

Imagine a hominin band resting near some trees, close to the shore of a shallow lake. No one relaxes, for a nearby pride of lions feasts on two zebras killed as the afternoon sun lengthens. As the sun nears the horizon, the lions move away. The hominins walk cautiously toward the kill, then break into a run, alert for hyenas and other predators after the same prey. Men and women alike pounce on the dismembered carcasses, cutting away meat and breaking open bones, then scamper away toward some trees by the lake. They swing rapidly into the branches, but an older male moves too slowly. A lion chases him, knocks him down, his jaws crunching the fugitive into bloody fragments. The beast stops for a moment, tail twitching in triumph, the carcass dangling from his jaws. Then he moves away. The hominins gesture helplessly, eat their scavenged meat, and life goes on.

FURTHER READING

The literature is enormous. Here are a few favorites. Louise Humphrey and Chris Stringer, *Our Human Story* (London: Natural History Museum, 2018) is an excellent summary for lay people. Chris Stringer and Peter Andrews, *The Complete Book of Human*

Evolution (London: Thames & Hudson, 2005) is a lavishly illustrated survey. Richard Klein, *The Human Career*, 3rd ed. (Chicago: University of Chicago Press, 2009) is an advanced textbook. Please beware that research moves ahead so fast that the only way to keep fully up to date is to follow the complex periodical literature, a task that challenges even experts!

2

OUT OF AFRICA (C. 2 MA AND LATER)

Schöningen, northern Germany, autumn, c. 300,000 to 400,000 years ago... People had preyed on the game that came to the shallow lake for thousands of years. Their camps lay in a temperate meadow and forest landscape, where stalkers could safely hide. On this occasion, the hunters watch a small herd of wild horses grazing close to the reeds at the water's edge. The beasts are alert for predators. Approaching them takes hours of patient movement, long hunting spears in hand. Two youths look at one another, stand upright quickly, and cast their carefully tapered wooden spears with deadly accuracy. The weapons twirl in flight, with enough force to stop two fleeing, wounded horses in their tracks. Other hunters move in and kill the flailing beasts as the herd gallops away. The band skins and dismembers the quarry, alert for hyenas and other hungry animals. Snow soon covers the butchered carcasses, the bones preserved by rising waters in spring.

FLUCTUATING ICE AGE CLIMATE

The Ice Age began about 2.5 Ma after an intensification of glaciation worldwide. Climatic fluctuations between warmer and colder climatic conditions were still relatively minor for the next million years. This was when a more advanced human evolved in Africa and moved out of the tropics into Asia and Europe.

DOI: 10.4324/9781003177326-2

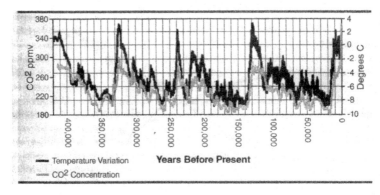

Figure 2.1 Ice Age climate change. Climatic fluctuations over the past 420,000 years, as revealed by the Vostok ice core, Antarctica, showing both temperature and CO₂ variations.

A major change took hold after about 780,000 years ago, when the earth's magnetic field shifted abruptly. Irregular climatic shifts followed for the rest of the Ice Age, recorded in deep sea and glacier cores. At least nine glacial episodes occurred, separated by shorter, more temperate conditions (interglacials). Experts believe that the world's climate has been in transition from one extreme to the other for at least 75 percent of the past 780,000 years. (For the past 420,000 years, see Figure 2.1)

The environmental changes were dramatic, with a major glacial period around 525,000 years ago, when ice extended as far south as Seattle, St. Louis, and New York in North America. Global sea levels were as much as 197 meters below modern levels. During glacial maxima, ice sheets covered a full third of the earth's surface. Sea levels fell dramatically as a result, rising close to modern shorelines during warmer interglacials. Much less is known about climatic shifts in tropical regions, but the southern margins of Africa's Sahara Desert expanded considerably during cold periods.

These climatic shifts played a major role in the spread of human beings through the temperate and tropical world after 2 Ma.

HOMO ERECTUS ("UPRIGHT PERSON")

In 1891, a Dutch surgeon, Eugène Dubois, discovered some bones from a thick-skulled human in Java (now Indonesia), which he described as *Pithecanthropus erectus*, "ape-human who stood upright".

Dubois was obsessed with the legendary "Missing Link" between apes and humans. He claimed that his discovery was the long sought-after link and was ridiculed for his pains. He reacted by withdrawing from science and is said to have kept his fossils under his bed.

Modern science has vindicated Dubois, also renamed his finds and other human fossils from Southeast Asia *Homo erectus*. The label is widely used, although a strong possibility exists that there are several forms, among them *Homo ergaster* ("the workman") from Africa and *Homo georgicus* from eastern Europe. Debates over the diversity of *Homo erectus* are unresolved. So we speak of African, Asian, and European examples of *Homo erectus*.

The successors to early *Homo* evolved in Africa, about 2 Ma and thrived there until around 1.5 Ma. We know little about their ancestry, but their skulls and jaws remain more primitive, while, from the neck down, their bones are, notably, modern looking. It seems that different parts of the human body evolved at varying rates, the body achieving fully modern form before the head. These Africans had body proportions relatively similar to ours. They were people with skulls and jawbones that displayed considerable variation. Some had modest brain sizes in the 508 to 550 cc range, while others had much larger brains with capacities of between 804 and 909 cc. Those with larger ones tended to possess well developed bony ridges above their eyes, wide nasal openings, and projecting mid-faces.

Whatever their brain size and facial appearance, African *Homo erectus* was slender and sometimes as tall as 1.85 meters. Arms were shorter, legs longer than earlier hominin species. Most likely, they spent all their time on the ground, walking and running very much like modern humans. Their spinal cord was narrower than in modern humans, as if the nervous system may not have been developed enough to control speech.

African *Homo erectus* flourished over a wide area from South Africa through East Africa's Great Rift Valley and beyond. We know this from their more elaborate stone tool technology, which dates back to at least 1.65 Ma. The toolmakers still relied on choppers and flakes. They also made an impressive array of new tools flaked from both sides to form straight-edged, pointed handaxes and straight-ended cleavers. These tools, seemingly used mainly for butchering game, required considerable skill and planning to manufacture (see Figure 2.2).

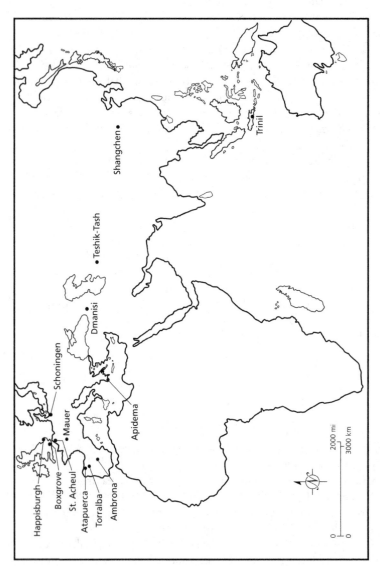

Figure 2.2 Map showing sites mentioned in Chapter 2.

Homo erectus flourished in hot, arid environments, probably the first humans that were nearly hairless, for they would not have sweated efficiently if covered with body hair. These were highly adaptable people, who covered long distances and moved over large home territories. They were the first humans to fashion more elaborate tools, to use fire, and to leave Africa.

LEAVING AFRICA AND THE "MUDDLE IN THE MIDDLE" (1.9 MA ONWARD)

It can be no coincidence that the first human settlement of cooler latitudes took hold after *Homo erectus* evolved in tropical Africa and mastered fire well over a million years ago. Fire protected bands against predators, warded off cold, and allowed hunters to pick off game fleeing from natural or deliberately set fires. Carrying simple fire brands for protection and lighting fires allowed people to move safely around open terrain and to expand more confidently into unfamiliar habitats, including higher ground.

Most important of all, fire gave people the ability to cook food, making it easier to eat and to extract more calories from foods of all kinds. The nutritional benefits were significant. Higher meat intake and cooked food may have led to an increase in brain size to about 1000 cc around 1.8 Ma years ago.

Quite why and when *Homo erectus* left tropical Africa is a mystery, largely because we lack sites that document any migration. By all appearances, they lived in small, highly mobile bands, just like their remote ancestors. Survival depended on mobility and by adapting to irregular changes between savanna, forest and desert. They would have migrated with changing vegetational zones, as other mammals did. Diets changed from meat to plant foods as they moved into unfamiliar landscapes. Finally, perhaps thanks to fire, they moved out of tropical latitudes into habitats never before occupied by humans (Figure 2.2).

These Africans were omnivores, eating both plants and animals, thus linked ecologically with other predators. There was widespread interchange of mammals between Africa and more temperate latitudes during the early Ice Age, which intensified after 700,000 years ago. For instance, the Sahara may have acted like a form of pump, sucking in humans and animals during wetter millennia and forcing them out northward and eastward to the margins of the desert and beyond during drier cycles. Most likely, the first successful human settlement of tropical Asia and temperate Europe coincided with radiations of mammalian communities out of Africa.

SETTLING ASIA (C. 2.1 MA AND LATER)

We know that early *Homo's* successors left Africa. The details still elude us, thanks to a persistent lack of human fossils. What, then, do we know? First, the Asian fossils. Except for the classic *Homo erectus* finds of over a century ago, the record is thin on the ground. *Erectus* fossils from the Trinil area of Java date to between 1.8 Ma and 60,0000 years ago. Others from northern and southern China date between 600,000 and 350,000 years ago, perhaps older. Skulls, jaws, and teeth tell us that the Asian populations were large-bodied and fully bipedal. They had relatively large brains, well-developed brow ridges and wide cheekbones. Most likely, their vision was excellent and some stood as tall as 1.8 meters. Whether there are earlier human settlers is uncertain, but, if they were, they were in very small numbers.

There are scatters of stone tools that tell of earlier settlement. Those from Shangchen in China date to about 2.1 Ma. Interestingly, the stone toolkits of Asian bands do not include the diagnostic handaxes or cleavers found in the west. This may be because of their need to adapt to a broad array of environments, including the harsh climate of northern China, or because of a greater reliance on forest woods like bamboo.

INHABITING EUROPE (C. 1.8 MA AND LATER)

The earliest human populations in Europe were also sparse. The earliest settlement is known from two widely spaced locations. Dmanisi in eastern Europe's Georgia has yielded a series of fragmentary human remains which date to about 1.8 Ma. No one knows whether these finds are an early form of *Homo erectus* or are the remains of an earlier human. They were originally named *Homo georgicus*, but are now categorized under *Homo erectus*.

Far to the west, the earliest known human skull comes from Sima del Elefante cave in the Atapuerca mountains near Burgos in northern Spain, dating to about 1.1 to 1.2 Ma. However, settlement, probably from the east, was sporadic at best in the harsh climatic conditions of the time.

The earliest lengthy European settlement dates to between 600,000 and 500,000 years ago. The newcomers were archaic humans with large, projecting faces, chinless, with massive jaws, large brow ridges and teeth, and flattened foreheads. Spanish anthropologists have named them *Homo antecessor*, arguing that these people were the shared ancestor of both Neanderthals and modern humans.

But *antecessor* has competition from *Homo heidelbergensis*, first known from a jawbone discovered at Mauer, Germany, a century ago. Most likely, *heidelbergensis* evolved from African *Homo erectus*, perhaps during the first expansion of humans out of Africa some 2 million years ago. The first appearance of *H. heidelbergensis* in Europe coincides with the arrival of stone handaxes, which had developed in Africa as early as 1.7 Ma. Subsequently, the newcomers evolved in both Europe and Africa. Little is known of their build, but they were compact people, with wide chests and much more human faces. Their brains were larger than those of African *Homo erectus*. Most experts believe that *Homo heidelbergensis* was the ancestor of the Neanderthals, but conclusive proof from either genetics or fossil bones remains in the future. Small wonder they refer to this chapter in human evolution as "the muddle in the middle."

By 400,000 years ago, human settlement was relatively widespread across western and Central Europe. The remains of between 32 and 59 individuals have come from the Sima de los Huesos cave, also at Atapuerca, dated to at least 300,000 years ago. All of them are *Homo heidelbergensis*, their bodies apparently dumped into a natural fissure.

ADEPT HUNTERS

Homo erectus was a far more sophisticated hunter than earlier humans, who relied heavily on scavenging. These were expert, big-game hunters with highly effective but simple hunting weapons and butchery toolkits. Some of their descendants (likely *H. antecessor*) are known from around one million years ago, from flint tools and footprints, discovered at Happisburgh in Norfolk, England. At Box-grove, Sussex, in the south of England, a cliff about 100 meters high overlooked a shallow lake fed by a spring. Around 500,000 years ago, people (this time of the *H. heidelbergensis* species) killed and butchered bison, bear, deer and wild horses at the foot of the cliff. One horse shoulder blade bears a hole made by a wooden spear.

Enormous quantities of meat came from the thoroughly butchered Boxgrove kills. The hunters dried both meat and skins for later use on a large scale. These were eclectic hunters, who hunted and scavenged, while also consuming plant foods.

Some 300,000 to 400,000 years ago, in what is now Germany, the aforementioned Schöningen stalkers relied on remarkably sophisticated weaponry. Their waterlogged archaeological sites have preserved finely crafted wooden spears, most of them fashioned from spruce, each made from small trees and measuring up to 2.5 meters long. Their owners chopped off the bark and branches, using the hardest wood at the base of the tree for the tip. The maximum thickness and weight lay a third of the way up the carefully trimmed shaft. This created a highly effective hunting weapon that had a range of about 60 meters with good penetrating power. The hunters may also have used wooden throwing sticks to bag geese which lived in the reeds around the site. Just as they had at Boxgrove, the people sliced meat into strips for drying.

Two swampy valleys at Ambrona and Torralba near Madrid, Spain have yielded the remains of dismembered elephants either driven into the muddy water, or enmired during spring and fall migrations. Without skeletal remains at either site, human presence (perhaps *H. heidelbergensis*) is identified by the stone tools and butchery marks on elephant bones—and through correlation with other sites of a similar age.

Everything at the site must have depended on careful observation, cautious stalking, also cooperation between bands large and small, varying with the season of the year and game movements. If these were members of the *Homo heidelbergensis* species, then we know from other findspots they would have had a larger brain with a more developed Broca's area, the zone associated with speaking ability. Some form of speech had come into use, but probably not nearly as complex as that of today.

HANDAXES AND OTHER TOOLS

Between 1.8 Ma and 150,000 years ago, the Acheulian handaxe (named after St. Acheul, a town in France) was one of the most widely distributed tools made by *Homo erectus* and its early successors.

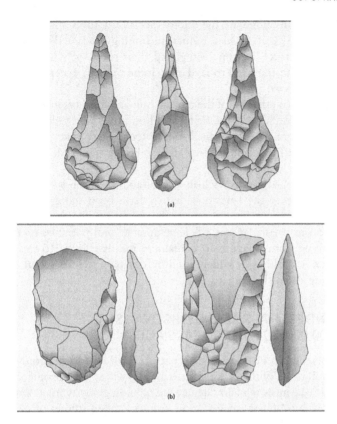

Figure 2.3 Handaxe technology. (a) Acheulian handaxe from Swanscombe, England (one-third actual size) (b) Two Acheulian cleavers from Angola and Zambia (both one-half actual size). Cleavers are thought to have been butchering tools. Their single unfinished edge has been shown by modern experiments to be effective for skinning and dismembering game.

By 700,000 years ago or so, Acheulian handaxe makers were achieving a degree of standardization unimaginable in earlier times. Clearly, the toolmakers had a clear mental image of the ideal end product, using a geometric sense of proportion accurately imposed on stone. They would first rough out the tool, flaking from both sides, then use a bone or wood striker to finish off the tool with straight edges and a sharp point (Figure 2.3).

There were none of the more specialized tools made during the later Ice Age. Archaic human technology lacked devices used for specific tasks. No one integrated their tools, of whatever raw material, with the need to feed and clothe oneself, except at a very generalized level.

The eastern portions of the archaic human world lay in Asia. One would logically expect the first Asian hominins, being ultimately of African origin, to bring the handaxe technology that was widely used in their homeland. Instead, they relied on far cruder choppers than the finely made axe.

Asian tropical forests, rich in animal and plant foods, are widely distributed over the landscape. It may have been more logical for people to rely on bamboo, wood, and other fibrous materials. Bamboo in particular was efficient, durable, and portable, used for everything from weapons to containers and dwellings. To this day, bamboo scaffolding is widely used by our own species when constructing Asian skyscrapers.

NEANDERTHALS AND DENISOVANS (C. 400,000 TO ?30,000 YEARS AGO)

Our perception of Neanderthals persists from a century ago. Many of us still think of the Neanderthals as dim-witted cave people. Even today, cartoonists regularly depict the men dragging women around by their hair. These images come from mistaken studies of elderly and disabled Neanderthals in the early 20th century. Today, *Homo neanderthalis* is the best known of all the archaic humans. They are known from thousands of fossil fragments, from premature fetuses to the very elderly.

Ignorant cave people? Wrong! Neanderthals were strong, robustly built humans with some archaic features. Their skulls display retreating foreheads, projecting faces, and sometimes prominent eyebrow ridges when compared with modern people. There are, of course, striking anatomical differences between Neanderthals and modern *Homo sapiens*, notably in Europe, where they had robust, squat bodies and immense strength. They were accomplished, nimble hunters, capable of considerable intellectual reasoning.

Researchers have managed to extract DNA from the first Neanderthal arm bone discovered in Germany's Neander Valley in 1856.

From this beginning, the geneticists have managed to sequence the Neanderthal genome. Neanderthal DNA differs from that of modern humans by about 27 or 28 base pairs. (These are the chemicals that form the fundamental units of the genetic code.) In contrast, modern human sequences in the same region of DNA differ from one another by only about 8 base points. Chimpanzees differ from modern human DNA by a much greater figure, about 55 base points. The geneticists have concluded that Neanderthals and moderns did not evolve from one another, but are distant relatives. Thus, Neanderthals were a distinct species, not a subspecies of anatomically modern *Homo sapiens*.

However, it does seem that our own species did interbreed with Neanderthals after some of us left our African homeland. Geneticists have established that all living humans (*Homo sapiens*) whose ancestry developed outside sub-Saharan Africa (where there were no Neanderthals) have between one and four percent of Neanderthal genome. This interbreeding is estimated to have occurred about 50,000 years ago, perhaps in Southwest Asia. As to our connection with the Neanderthals, we are two separate species, who shared a common ancestor perhaps 700,000 years ago. The identity of this ancestor is unclear, but it may have been *H. heidelbergensis*.

The evolutionary plot thickens even more. Far to the northeast, a human finger bone unearthed in Denisova Cave in the Altai region of Siberia yielded DNA that showed that these little known "Denisovans" were more closely linked to the Neanderthals. They diverged from them about 300,000 to 400,000 years ago. We still know little about the Denisovans, who visited the cave from about 200,000 to 50,000 years ago. There are signs that both Neanderthals and a still unknown more archaic human interbred with them—as did *Homo sapiens*. Today's people from Papua New Guinea and other Melanesians in the Pacific have an average of 4.8 percent Denisovan genomes. But how did Denisovans get there? Did they engage in ocean seafaring? DNA tells us little about behavior or intelligence, which can only come from fossils that are, so far, elusive. The search for Denisovans is intensifying, among other places in China.

Neanderthals, Denisovans, *Homo sapiens*, and maybe other, still unknown, human forms: this intriguing tapestry of evolving ancestors formed a series of evolutionary lineages that survived, and changed over hundreds of millennia. There may have been interbreeding, but the different species remained distinct. In the end, they all became extinct except for us, the anatomically modern humans, *Homo sapiens*.

INTRODUCING NEANDERTHALS

Almost all that we know about the Neanderthals as people comes from their classic homelands in Southwest Asia and Europe. Neanderthals flourished throughout Europe and Southwest Asia by 350,000 to around 30,000 years ago. They had an upright posture, and the same manual abilities, range, and movement abilities as modern people. They differed in having massive limb bones, often somewhat bowed in the thighs and forearms, reflecting their greater muscular power. Their brain capacity ranged between 1200 to 1750 cc (compared to the 1000–2000 cc range of *Homo sapiens*). Indeed, their average cranial capacity was 1475 cc, which is slightly larger than our own average. There was considerable anatomical variability. European Neanderthals, habitually living in extremely cold environments, were squat people, with massive brow ridges; but they were as nimble as modern humans, standing about 1.52 to 1.68 meters tall (Figures 2.4 and 2.5).

Like their predecessors, Neanderthal bands occupied large territories. Their members were skilled hunters, who pursued large game like the mammoth (the long-haired arctic elephant), also wild oxen, reindeer, and wild horses. They also caught birds and fish and used their impressive knowledge of the landscape to exploit a wide range of plant foods. For all this diversity, theirs was a precarious existence. In winter, European Neanderthals used caves and rock shelters. During the warmer months, they fanned out over more open country, living in temporary camps.

Much depended on a close knowledge of animal habits and on refined hunting skills. Stalking was all-important, given that the weaponry at their disposal was little more than stone-tipped spears and throwing sticks. Much successful hunting depended on cooperative ambushes of beasts like reindeer migrating in spring or fall. Hunters literally had to come within such close range that they could almost touch their prey. Judging from injuries to Neanderthal skeletons, they clubbed or wrestled their kill to the ground, often receiving injuries like those of modern-day rodeo riders. In many respects they were predators at the summit of their ecosystem.

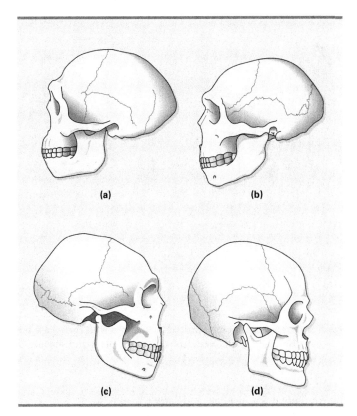

Figure 2.4 Neanderthals and modern humans. (a) and (b). Classic Neanderthal skulls with prominent brow ridges, a bun-shaped rear to the skull and a retreating chin. (c) a Neanderthal from Shanidar cave in Iraq has a higher forehead and somewhat reduced brow ridges. (d) a modern skull for comparison.

Above all, Neanderthals were opportunistic hunters and foragers, especially after 50,000 years ago. This may have been the time when technology became more organized, when planning the hunt assumed greater importance. Much hunting in Europe focused on four main herd animals—bison, horse, red deer, and reindeer. Targeting these animals with ambushes yielded considerable amounts of meat. The people may have hunted to dry flesh and store it for use during the cold winter months.

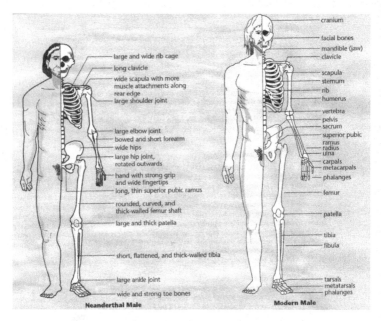

Figure 2.5 A skeleton of a Neanderthal (left) compared with that of a modern human (right). The Neanderthal is more robust and skinnier than the modern.

Environmental knowledge and larger group sizes were keys to long-term survival. Every band relied on predictable movements of game and seasons of edible plant foods, as interregional differences appeared in the Neanderthal world. For instance, the deep river valleys of southwestern France were inhabited year-round, while people exploited open plains to the north during the warmer months.

NEANDERTHAL TECHNOLOGY AND BELIEFS

Neanderthal technology was more complex than the handaxe-based toolkits of earlier times. While the basic tools remained relatively simple, there were technological advances. Unlike their ancestors, Neanderthal toolmakers prepared stone lumps as pre-forms that determined the shape of the flake or flakes removed from them. Prepared cores with flattened tops (known as Levallois cores, after the Paris suburb where they were first discovered) produced single large flakes and triangular points with lethally sharp edges (Figure 2.6).

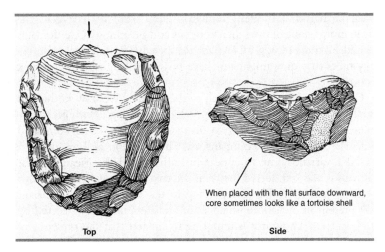

When placed with the flat surface downward, core sometimes looks like a tortoise shell

Top   Side

Figure 2.6 A carefully prepared "Levallois" core, which produced a thin, very
    sharp flake.

In contrast, disc-shaped cores produced as many flakes of different sizes as possible. These technologies produced spear points and
scraping tools, the latter used for both woodworking and skin processing. The toolmakers sharpened the edges of their points and
scrapers with small, steplike chips created by careful trimming.

There are major regional variations in Neanderthal toolkits,
known generally as "Mousterian", after the Le Moustier rock shelters
in Southwest France. These differences need not concern us here,
for Mousterian technology was fundamentally very simple, with few
formal tools. Edge wear studies tell us that many people used stone
flakes for cutting and scraping. They simply picked up a conveniently
shaped piece, used it to skin or butcher, or to cut thongs, then threw
it away. Nevertheless, the Neanderthals developed tools for different activities more quickly than their forebears, perhaps at a time of
growing human populations and slightly enhanced social complexity.

Neanderthals were hunter-gatherers at a time when the world's
human population was still small, but life was becoming gradually
more complex. Important questions about them remain unanswered.
Did they have language (the mental process of communication) and
speech (the externalization of it) and pass complex information from
one generation to the next? Speech and language are intangible, so
they can only be studied indirectly. The hypoglossal canal, which
carries the nerves from the brain to the tongue are equivalent in

Neanderthals and modern humans. They seem to have had the same motor control over their tongues and breathing as we do. But, despite all these biological features for speech, Neanderthal technology hints that they might not have possessed language as complex as ours.

Genetic analysis is also adding to the picture. We now know that the FOXP2 gene is involved in speech and language. Both Neanderthals and *Homo sapiens* share two changes in this gene when compared with the sequence in chimpanzees. The question is, how did this FOXP2 variant come to appear in both us and the Neanderthals? Perhaps it was transferred between the two species via gene flow, or perhaps (and more likely, according to the researchers) this variant was present in our common ancestor and then favorably selected by both species. Though it is tempting to suggest that the presence of the same haplotype in both Neanderthals and us means that Neanderthals had similarly complex language capabilities as our own, there is still not enough evidence to draw this conclusion. Genes are just one factor of many in the development of language.

Nor are there signs of any form of the complex symbolic beliefs articulated by *Homo sapiens*, with only a few notable exceptions: some Neanderthals buried their dead. Two adults and four children were discovered buried close together in a camp site in the La Ferrassie rockshelter in southwestern France. A band of Siberian goat hunters buried a child in a shallow pit at Teshik-Tash cave in the western foothills of the Himalayas. Six pairs of mountain goat horns lay atop the grave. Whether these burials were mere corpse disposal or associated with beliefs in an afterlife is a matter for debate.

But some Neanderthals were certainly cannibals. A cave occupied by Neanderthals at Moula-Guercy in France about 100,000 years ago has yielded human skulls broken to get at the brain, and limb bones bearing clear signs of butchery and de-fleshing. Those who dismembered them processed the bones just like those of animals. Likewise, there is some evidence that Neanderthals may have engaged in artistic endeavors—for example, the possible use of bird feathers and claws as personal ornaments. Although the evidence is still far from definitive, such research is opening up the possibility of symbolic behavior among the Neanderthals.

The Neanderthals' increasingly sophisticated culture mirrors some early glimpses of our own complicated beliefs, societies and religious sense. They seem to have lived in cooperative, compassionate groups. The skull of an elderly man (aged around 40, but he had endured a hard life) from the La Chapelle-aux-Saints cave in France had lost many teeth, and would presumably have needed caring support to survive, which he must have received.

THE MYSTERY OF EXTINCTION

European Neanderthals became extinct sometime between 40,000 and 30,000 years ago. The date is much debated, but one thing is certain: for several thousand years, Neanderthals and incoming *Homo sapiens* lived in Europe alongside one another before the former became extinct. That there were contacts between Neanderthals and newcomers seems certain, for there are sites in France and northern Spain where the distinctive tools of both groups appear in the same caves, stratified one above the other so closely that they must have alternated visitations there.

The moment *Homo sapiens* spread across Europe some time before 40,000 years ago, the Neanderthals were at a disadvantage. They were no slouches, but, as we shall see, the weaponry of the newcomers was lighter and more efficient. Above all, they seem to have lacked the qualities of imagination, self-awareness, or the planning abilities found in moderns. Nor did they possess the complex social mechanisms that fostered innovation and the effortless passage of knowledge from one generation to the next. This is not to suggest that we killed them off: one geneticist notes that their numbers had been dwindling from at least 100,000 years ago, long before *Homo sapiens* permanently entered their homelands, likely the consequence of a worsening climate.

Extinction was probably a slow death, where the Neanderthals gradually withdrew to the margins. Neanderthal populations must have become more and more isolated to the point where all childbearing women died and band after band slowly vanished. There is no evidence for some decisive, bloody encounter between "them" and "us", rather that their extinction seems to have been down to a combination of falling numbers, perhaps impacted by the climate, and perhaps also competition with increasingly numerous modern humans.

★ ★ ★

The Neanderthals have long vanished, but deserve our profound respect. Imagine a summer's day in Central Europe 45,000 years ago. Three young Neanderthal hunters lie in a forest clearing. They haven't moved in hours, their eyes never leaving the solitary male bison grazing peacefully on the young grass. The oldest, and most experienced, clasps a short-handled spear and rises silently to his feet close to the rear flank of the unsuspecting beast. He jumps lightly onto the bison's back and plunges his spear between its shoulders. His quarry bellows and rears as he hangs on to the spear and twists it back and forth in the bleeding wound. The huntsman tumbles to the ground as the bison tramples on him and breaks his arm. The hunter's companions cast spears into the rearing quarry as it charges blindly into the trees. They follow the weakened prey as it stumbles and falls by a nearby riverbank, where they dispatch it with brutal spear thrusts.

Such hunting requires extraordinary knowledge, vast experience, and a familiarity with formidable prey. Kills required virtually touching the animal, not the luxury of telescopic sights and a rifle shot.

FURTHER READING

The references listed in Chapter 1 are excellent introductions. Neanderthals: Dimitra Papagianni and Michael A. Morse, *Neanderthals Rediscovered: How Modern Science is Rewriting Their Story*, rev. ed. (London and New York: Thames & Hudson, 2015) is a well-illustrated introduction. A popular account: Rebecca Wragg Sykes, *Kindred: Neanderthal Life, Love, Death and Art* (New York: Times Books, 2020). Tom Higham, *The World Before Us: How Science is Revealing a New Story of our Human Origins* (New Haven: Yale University Press, 2021) is an eloquent account of what we know about the Denisovans. For an in-depth account of ancient DNA by one of the chief researchers, we recommend *Who We Are and How We Got Here* by David Reich (Oxford: Oxford University Press, 2018).

3

ENTER *HOMO SAPIENS* (C. 300,000 YEARS AGO AND LATER)

Border Cave, on the margins of what is now South Africa and ESwatini (Swaziland), 170,000 years ago... The women are sorting through large bundles of freshly uprooted *Hypoxia* stems, dug up with wooden sticks and sharpened bones piled nearby. Nearby, fast burning firewood collapses into fine ash, where small piles of fresh, green nutty vegetables are roasting. Their surfaces split as the moisture escapes. While the ashes cool, the hungry people rake the cooked rhizomes from the hearth.

Hypoxis is not exactly a household word. But *Hypoxis angustifolia* has been a prized African comfort food for tens of thousands of years. It's a rhizome, a subterranean plant stalk that produces thumb-sized, starchy root vegetables that can be eaten raw or roasted in ashes. Many of these plants can be harvested at one time and carried in bundles back to camp. Easily collected and roasted, this invaluable staple grows along the eastern flank of tropical Africa and into Yemen in the Arabian Peninsula and is still widely eaten today. Cooking makes *Hypoxis* easy to peel and eat. It releases glucose and breaks down the fiber, which makes the rhizomes easier to digest. Apart from being easy to carry on the move, the food was much easier for the elderly and the young to consume.

DOI: 10.4324/9781003177326-3

The Border Cave *Hypoxis* are the earliest known cooked plant foods in the world.

HOMO SAPIENS (MODERN HUMANS, *C.* 300,000 YEARS AGO—PRESENT)

We call ourselves *Homo sapiens,* "wise person". We are clever people, capable of subtlety, of manipulation, and of self-understanding. We modern humans are very adaptable, successful primates, found on every continent and the only surviving hominin of the past 6 million-plus years. While we emerged before 300,000 years ago, at first, our skulls show a mix of archaic and modern traits. We only became fully skeletally modern by perhaps 120,000 years ago. Such *Homo sapiens* would have been physically (and presumably cerebrally) identical to any modern human, and are known in the literature as AMH which stands for "anatomically modern humans" (while the precise scientific label, not used in this book, is *Homo sapiens sapiens*—double the wise).

What separates us from earlier humans? The answers are complicated and not always obvious, particularly since various other hominins have possessed similar traits to our own—from upright stances to big brains, to the FOXP2 gene associated with speech and language. Rather than comparing, perhaps the answer is to consider what many believe to be our greatest asset: articulate, fluent speech. We communicate, we tell stories, we pass on knowledge and ideas, all through the medium of language. Consciousness, cognition, self-awareness, foresight, and the ability to express oneself and one's emotions are direct consequences of fluent speech. They are also linked to our capacity for symbolic and spiritual thought. We're concerned not just with subsistence and technology, but also with the boundaries of existence, and the relations between the individual, the group, and the universe.

With these abilities and the full flowering of human creativity expressed in art and religion, *Homo sapiens* eventually colonized not just temperate and tropical environments, but the entire globe.

OUR ORIGINS (*C.* 300,000 YEARS AGO)

For generations, two opposing theories sought to explain the origins of modern humans.

REGIONAL CONTINUITY MODEL

This scenario argued that *Homo erectus* evolved independently in different regions of the Old World, first into intermediary forms of humans and then into fully modern people. In other words, there were multiple, ancient, origins for different regional groups of humans. Meanwhile, highly adaptive, novel anatomical features spread rapidly. These kept human populations on the same fundamental evolutionary path toward modern people.

OUT OF AFRICA MODEL

This approach argues that *Homo sapiens* evolved in Africa and then spread elsewhere from what was a single place of origin. It argues that today's geographic populations have shallow roots derived from a single source in relatively recent times.

After years of research into genetics and archaeology, consensus holds that the Out of Africa theory is correct, but with some modifications. All *Homo sapiens* are indeed of recent African origin, but that they engaged with some minor interbreeding with now-extinct human species: both within Africa, and—for those who left Africa—with the Neanderthals and Denisovans (if not others, too).

Molecular biology has played a major role in unraveling modern human origins. Researchers initially zeroed in on mtDNA (mitochondrial DNA), which mutates much faster than nuclear DNA. This mtDNA is inherited only through the maternal line and does not mix with paternal DNA, which means it provides a potentially reliable link with ancestral populations. The latest research tells us that the mtDNA lineage evolved for some time in Africa, followed by an out-migration by a small number of people. All later Asian and European *Homo sapiens* lineages originated in this small African population.

When did the most common recent ancestor live? Molecular biology dated the split to about 200,000 years ago. This date is a statistical approximation. The fossil evidence comprises a scatter of *Homo sapiens* finds in sub-Saharan Africa, specifically from Omo Kibish and Herto in Ethiopia from a time bracket between 195,000 and 150,000 years ago. Specialists have also found skull fragments from the Apidima Cave in Greece, which have been controversially dated to at least 210,000 years ago. Finally, there are some even earlier *Homo sapiens* individuals from Jebel Irhoud cave in Morocco in northwestern Africa dating to about 315,000 years ago.

A mere scatter of human fossils, but there are other interesting clues. Between 200,000 and 100,000 years ago, the age-old handaxe technology of earlier times gave way to lighter toolkits in eastern and southern Africa that combined sharp stone flakes with wooden spear shafts and more specialized tools for woodworking and butchery. Perhaps these lighter, but simple, tools were the remote prototypes of more efficient ones that developed after 75,000 years ago.

All the available information points to an African homeland for our species, *Homo sapiens*. But tens of thousands of years passed before AMHs explored new continents.

MOVING OUT OF AFRICA (C. 120,000 YEARS AGO AND LATER)

There was no one moment when a band of anatomically modern humans (AMH) woke up one day in Africa and decided to travel far from home. We will never decipher the details of what must have been irregular and sporadic population movements, most of them dictated by the realities of life as a hunter and forager (Figure 3.1). Putting the contested early Greek evidence to one side for now, the oldest AMH remains found outside Africa have come from two caves in Israel dating to about 120,000 to 90,000 years ago. These individuals were thin on the ground and living in the same landscapes as Neanderthals, with whom they occasionally interbred. They left few traces of their presence there, which is hardly surprising, given their small numbers. We only have widespread indications of AMH settlement around 50,000 years ago.

There may have been few of them, but the newcomers were accustomed to maintaining connections with fellow kin and neighbors over long distances. Their weaponry was light and efficient for tackling animals large and small, while they also relied on a wide range of plant foods. These were people adapted to semi-arid and arid landscapes where survival depended on information exchanged with others.

The Nile Valley was a natural route to the north, with the Sahara Desert a seemingly major barrier to movement toward the

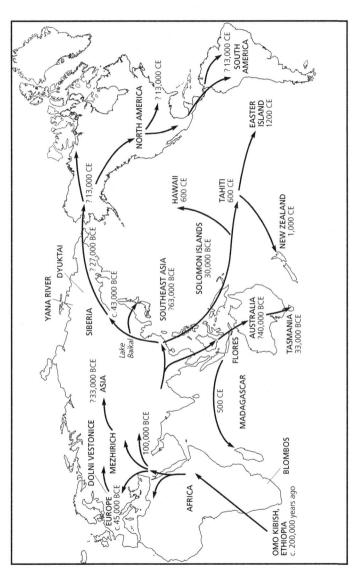

Figure 3.1 The spread of modern humans.

Mediterranean. But bitterly cold conditions during the last glaciation in the north brought a cooler and wetter climate to the Sahara from before 100,000 until about 40,000 years ago. For long periods, what is now one of the driest places on earth supported semi-arid grassland and herds of game. These were millennia when people could hunt and forage their way across the Sahara. They may have moved northward along now-dried-up watercourses leading from the heart of the desert. Others still are thought to have crossed over the narrow straits of the Red Sea, from Ethiopia (a heartland of our species) to the Arabian Peninsula, and thence onwards to the east. We know from stone tools found on the Red Sea plain of Arabia that archaic human species had been making this passage deep into the Ice Age.

AFRICA: THOSE WHO STAYED AT HOME (C. 65,000 YEARS AGO TO MODERN TIMES)

CONTINUITY

The genetic ancestry of indigenous sub-Saharan Africans goes back to the very beginnings of modern humanity. Some of the oldest genealogical lineages on earth lie among the Hazda of modern-day Tanzania, the Pygmies of the Congo, and the San of southern Africa. All of them were hunter-gatherers with deep roots in the remote past.

The first archaeological signs of modern cognition among *Homo sapiens* groups includes material found in the Blombos Cave in Southern Africa. Dated to before 70,000 years ago, it comprises shell beads and abstract, ocher-painted art. Other signs of modern human behavior appeared in southern Africa by at least 65,000 years ago. Tools and weapons became gradually smaller and more efficient and may even have included a simple bow-and-arrow. From the beginning, AMHs visited southern African caves like Klasies River and Sibudu as they gradually developed more efficient ways of hunting and foraging (Figure 3.2). Rainfall improved after 50,000 years ago; Africa's population grew rapidly. By then, AMHs flourished throughout sub-Saharan Africa.

At that time, our species lived off a wide range of game and plant foods, and, near coasts, off mollusks, fish, penguins, and seals.

Figure 3.2 Map showing sites in Chapter 3.

Hunters pursued more docile antelope like the eland. They exploited more formidable animals like buffalo and elephant, whose flesh may have been scavenged from predator kills, especially those of older or young beasts. By 13,000 years ago, just after the end of the last glaciation, hunting became more specialized, perhaps as more easily hunted animals became rarer owing to overhunting.

Even further south, close to modern-day Cape Town, the people visiting Elands Bay Cave took large and medium-sized antelope in 11,000 BCE. Two thousand years later, they turned their attention to smaller browsing animals and relied heavily on mollusks and marine animals. At first, hunting bands merely visited the cave, then lived there for long periods of time. Then, around 6000 BCE, they abandoned the cave as rising sea levels flooded the nearby coastal plain when the climate became warmer.

As temperatures warmed after the last glaciation, so the African interior became drier. Hunting and foraging became ever more specialized as people moved close to reliable water supplies and to coastal areas where herds of smaller animals might be found. Many groups, such as the rainforest peoples of the Congo Basin, were unable to hunt as many animals as those dwelling in woodland and savanna landscapes so they relied heavily on rabbits, tortoises, and also on plant foods.

Unfortunately, preservation conditions are such that most sites once occupied by these groups yield only stone tools and the occasional bone spear point. There are exceptions, like the Gwisho hot springs in Central Zambia, which lie on the edge of the seasonally flooded floodplain of the Kafue River. Several hunting camps nestled among the bubbling hot springs, which were occupied repeatedly for over 3000 years. The waterlogged levels of the camps contain not only the bones of animals of all sizes, but also plant remains, mostly from eight species, notably the edible seeds of the *Bauhinia* shrub. So little have foraging practices changed over the past 3000 years that a San from the Kalahari was able to identify seeds from the excavations and tell the archaeologists what they were used for.

There were traces of a grass-and-stick shelter, of hearths, and layers of grass that may have served as bedding. Thirty-five people were buried in the camps. Hundreds of stone arrow barbs and small scraping tools lay alongside pestles and grindstones used to process the plant foods that were central to the Gwisho diet. The people uprooted roots with wooden digging sticks found in the site. There were even the remains of plants used to poison arrow heads.

We cannot, of course, assume that the 3000 year-old Gwisho site was a prototype for modern lifeways, but the general similarities are striking. For example, the average present-day San camp in the Kalahari Desert holds between 10 and 30 people, just as the Gwisho camp probably did. If ancient San communities were anything like modern ones, a camp would have been in a continual state of social flux. Kinship systems among hunter-gathers tend to

Figure 3.3 San hunter-gatherers created rock paintings, like this one from South Africa. This scene had deep symbolic meaning that defies modern interpretation, but the human figures are elongated to depict an altered state of consciousness.

be highly flexible. Every member of a band has not only close family connections, but also kin ties with a much larger number of people living over a wide area. Such arrangements mean that individuals are able to move to a new camp and readily find a family with kin ties to accept them. Quite apart from preventing social chaos, such easy movement functions as a network for mutual assistance in times of food scarcity.

Ancient San paintings and engravings amplify what we know from archaeology and ethnographic studies of 19th-century and modern-day San groups. San artists depicted the game they hunted, the chase, and life in camp. They drew running hunters, people fishing from canoes, and scenes of gathering honey and plant foods (Figure 3.3). The hunters can be seen stalking game in disguise. In one example, a hunter wearing an ostrich skin stands in the midst of a flock of his prey.

One can justly admire San rock art as an artistic tradition in its own right, and with good reason. The artists were highly talented. But much San art has deeper symbolic meanings, some of which have come down to us from 19th-century research by German-born linguist Wilhelm Bleek. South African archaeologist David Lewis-Williams has studied these ethnographic records of San art. He points out that each superimposition of paintings, and each relationship between human figures and animals, had profound meaning to the artists and the people.

Many of the paintings depict eland antelope with dancers cavorting around them. Lewis-Williams believes that the dancers were acquiring the potency released by the death of their prey. Perhaps, he argues, they went into trances so powerful that they became eland themselves while in an altered state of consciousness. Lewis-Williams and others argue that shamanistic behavior with its trances and hallucinogenic drugs was involved, to the accompaniment of much scholarly controversy. This debate, like so many others, is unresolved.

By the end of the 19th century, there was no San painting in South Africa. The art of stone toolmaking had all but died out. The last stoneworkers used industrial glass bottle fragments instead of their usual quartz pebbles. In the face of African farming people, who spread into southern Africa after 1 CE, and then European settlement, they retreated from the savanna woodlands into remoter, and often drier, landscapes, where their descendants survive in ever smaller numbers to this day.

SPREADING TO THE EAST (C. 120,000 YEARS AGO AND LATER)

There is one certainty about AMH groups of 120,000 years ago and later. They moved irregularly and constantly. A territory could become too crowded; a band would split, its members heading in opposite directions; A young man and his family would move to a neighboring valley in search of game or plant foods. Distance was unimportant, but human connections provided information, as well as wives. The dynamics behind these seemingly irregular movements propelled AMHs to every corner of the world, and from Africa into Asia and beyond. For instance, as conditions in the Middle East grew progressively drier after 50,000 years ago while the last glaciation intensified in the north, the AMH newcomers responded to population pressure and food shortages by moving northward and northwestward in Europe and Eurasia, also westward along Mediterranean coasts (see Chapter 4).

The movement out of tropical Africa followed routes used down the ages, and saw people moving eastward, into and across the Nile Valley and the Red Sea, also across the narrow southern end of the Red Sea, over to the lower reaches of Arabia. Ultimately, they wound their ways into the subtropical and tropical reaches of South and Southeast Asia. Unfortunately, the details remain hazy, clues virtually non-existent. Forty-seven AMH teeth from Fuyan Cave in southern China date to between 120,000 and 80,000 years ago. Some stone tools dating to around 70,000 years ago come from the Malay peninsula. Most likely, some AMH bands had crossed India by that time, but this is little more than a guess. Whether there was but one permanent dispersal from Africa, or many of them, is unknown.

But the *Homo sapiens* were not alone at this early stage. There still existed other hominin species, including the mysterious diminutive humans from Flores island's Liang Bua cave, which date to between 100,000 and 50,000 years ago. They were only about a meter tall, with prominent brow ridges and a low brain case. The teeth are modern, the face delicate, but the limbs are slight. Named *Homo floresiensis*, they may be the descendants of a remnant *Homo erectus* population, who occupied the region very much earlier. As to their small stature, it was likely the result of dwarfism by isolation.

Although their disappearance roughly coincides with our appearance in the region, there is no evidence that we were the necessary cause of their demise. Instead, perhaps challenging climatic conditions were involved in their extinction. Around 70,000 years ago, Mount Toba, a major active volcano on Sumatra in Southeast Asia exploded in one of the greatest eruptions of the past 23 million years. Dense clouds of volcanic ash fell over a wide area from the northeastern Arabian Sea and much of the Indian Ocean, on northern India and Bangladesh, also the South China Sea. The eruption must have decimated animal and plant communities over a huge area of the tropics. As large eruptions always do, several years of colder weather and intense drought affected a wide area.

The Mount Toba cataclysm must have affected sparse human populations over thousands of square kilometers. Competing theories are emerging. At one extreme, some experts argue that the falling ash devastated human populations, many of them far from the volcano. A severe genetic bottleneck caused by the mass casualties took hold, impeding cultural development. But climatic data from cores bored into Lake Malawi in Central Africa indicate that the eruption did not impact East Africa significantly, and that the eruption did not cause a genetic bottleneck. Africa was a long way from Southeast Asia, so the effects of the disaster must have been muted.

Another plausible scenario talks not of genetic bottlenecks, but of a series of innovative "sparks" of rapid change in some areas, but not in others. One such spark was the development of blade technology in the Middle East by 50,000 years ago (see Chapter 4). The appearance of art in Europe and Southeast Asia between 40,000 and 50,000 years before present, perhaps also Africa, may have been another spark. It was only after about 30,000 years ago that rapid culture change took place in all parts of the humanly colonized world.

Full modern human behavior seems to have developed over a long period, perhaps in fits and starts, with fully articulate human speech as a major contributor. By 50,000 years, AMHs were firmly established, albeit in small numbers, in eastern and southwestern Asia. Thereafter, a complex process of colonization and dispersal carried their descendants into every kind of natural environment imaginable—to East and mainland Southeast Asia, to New Guinea, Australia, and the frontiers of the Pacific, also to Europe, Eurasia, and the Americas.

The geneticists are certain that modern humans settled Southeast Asia in multiple waves. They speculate that there may have been two movements. One involved some Denisovan DNA, contributing the ancestors of New Guineans and Australians among others. The second brought present-day East Asians and Indonesians.

GOING OFFSHORE: SUNDA AND SAHUL (AFTER 60,000 YEARS AGO)

This is all very tentative, whereas the geological evidence is not. At the height of the last glaciation about 18,000 years ago, global sea levels were over 90 meters below modern levels. Southeast Asia's geography was radically different. Dry land linked Sumatra to Borneo. Rolling plains connected to the Asian mainland linked many of the offshore islands. Great rivers crossed the now-submerged plains, forming a long-vanished land known to geologists as Sunda. Further offshore, another vast landmass called Sahul linked Australia, Tasmania, and New Guinea. The lower sea levels meant that open water passages were much shorter, but people still needed watercraft to colonize New Guinea and Australia.

Watercraft were essential to cross deep water, with most human settlement along coasts and close to reliable water supplies. Here the inhabitants could catch fish and mollusks, especially giant clams, in shallow water, as well as hunt game and harvest plant foods. Simple rafts of mangrove poles and bamboo lashed together with forest vines would have sufficed for fishing in shallow water and for reaching offshore shell beds. Such rafts may have been the way that people first crossed from the mainland to Sunda and Sahul, perhaps blown offshore by strong winds. For instance, computer simulations suggest that a raft could have drifted from the island of Timor to what is now Australia in a mere seven days.

This colonization took place remarkably quickly, between about 40,000 and 45,000 years ago. We know, for example, that tuna fishers visited Jerimalai Cave on East Timor at least 42,000 years ago. People had settled along some 3000 kilometers of the Sahul coastline soon afterward.

Much of Sahul was rolling, semi-arid lowlands (what is now Australia) with a quite different landscape of rugged mountains and highland valleys in the north. Genetic data hints that Australia and New Guinea were occupied about 55,000 years ago, with the earliest archaeological evidence for human settlement in New Guinea coming from the highlands about 45,000 years before present.

THE ARTISTS

For a century, archaeologists have been convinced that the world's earliest figurative (as opposed to abstract) art comes from European caves (see Chapter 4). But they may be wrong. The Leang Tedongnge cave on the island of Sulawesi, Indonesia, lies in a remote valley hemmed in by limestone cliffs; periodic flooding means that it is only accessible during the dry season. An unknown artist painted a dark red warty pig on the wall of the cave with red ocher pigment (Figure 3.4). The painting shows a short crest of upright hair, and a pair of hornlike facial warts that are characteristic of adult males. There are two handprints above the pig's hindquarters. It appears to be facing two other (only partially preserved) pigs, as if observing a fight or social interaction between them. Using uranium-series

Figure 3.4 Painting of a warty pig at Leang Tedongnge cave with accompanying hand impressions, Sulawesi, Indonesia, *c.* 45,500 years old.

Courtesy Maxime Aubert

isotope dating, expert Maxime Aubert dated the calcite layer overlying the painting to 45,500 years ago. This is a minimum date for the painting, which underlies the calcite, apparently the oldest cave painting in the world.

Dozens of caves on Sulawesi have yielded hands stencils, cave paintings, also pigment crayons, and carved figurines. One scene in red pigment in a small ceiling space depicting a hunting scene where eight hunters, armed with spears or ropes, pursue a Sulawesi warty hog and a small-horned dwarf buffalo, both of which still live on the island. They have elongated snouts, as if they were wearing masks. More likely the figures are mythical animal–human figures participating in a ritual hunt. A calcite layer overlying the paintings gives a minimum age of 44,000 years ago.

If the dates stand up to further scrutiny, this vibrant artistic tradition is at least 4000 years older than the dates given to any other figurative rock art in the world. It developed on the island soon after the first modern human settlement of about 50,000 years ago.

INTO THE PACIFIC

To the east of New Guinea lies open ocean, with islands close off-shore. The island of New Britain is only 50 kilometers further, with New Ireland a short voyage further on. Deep water separates the two islands, which may be seen from one another. Some form of seaworthy watercraft came into use for paddling from New Guinea. Voyages must have been commonplace by 35,000 years ago, by which time people were catching shark and tuna. By 20,000 years ago, their successors were trading fine-grained obsidian, a volcanic glass for toolmaking, across open water from nearby New Britain.

Some voyagers were even more ambitious. By 30,000 years ago, communities of islanders were catching tuna, mackerel and other open water fish while visiting Kilu rock shelter on Buka Island in the northern Solomon Islands. Fishing there would have required open water voyages of at least 130 to 180 kilometers. These would have involved not only seaworthy canoes, but also reliable water contain-ers and enough food for several days at sea.

Generally good weather, also predictable seasonal winds and cur-rents carried Ice Age voyagers this far offshore. This was the limit of their pioneer journeys, for distances to islands further out in the southwestern Pacific were much longer. Such passages required larger canoes, much more sophisticated navigational skills, and easily storable food crops. The closer islands were a superb "nursery" for seafaring techniques without elaborate technology.

AUSTRALIA

The first settlement of Australia is surrounded by controversy, just as is that over the first Americans (see Chapter 4). Human settlement is well documented after 36,000 to 38,000 years ago, but traces of earlier settlement are very thin. Once again, it's a matter of finding traces of very sparse, mobile hunter-gatherer groups.

A few traces of human settlement survive. Madjedbebe rock shel-ter lies in the Kakadu National Park in northern Australia. This site has yielded numerous well-dated stone tools, which are said to be at least 65,000 years old. The Warratyi rock shelter in the Flinders Ranges of South Australia has dates as early as 49,000 years ago. Lake Mungo in western New South Wales, again in the south, is said to date to about 40,000. The isolated finds from Madjedbebe and elsewhere hint at a virtually invisible occupation for many thousands of years.

Whatever the date of initial colonization, we know that people could have walked all the way from New Guinea to Tasmania far to the south throughout the late Ice Age. Some scholars believe that initial colonization was a slow, gradual process that unfolded along the coasts, then into the interior. Others argue for rapid colonization in small groups, who expanded rapidly over the continent as a result of their highly mobile lifeways.

In the far south, climatic conditions in Tasmania were quite severe, with ice sheets on higher ground. Low sea levels connected the island to the mainland for at least 55,000 years, so the first settlers simply walked there. There is well documented settlement as early as 35,000 years ago at the Parmerpar Meethaner Cave, which was occupied until about 780 years ago. People dwelt in the rugged landscape of Central Tasmania throughout the coldest millennia of the last glaciation around 18,000 years ago. Their main prey was red wallabies in a diet combined with plant foods. These were the southernmost people living on earth during the last glaciation.

Between 25,000 and 10,000 years ago, Australia's human population may have numbered as many as a million people. The Australian Aborigines maintained their traditional lifeway with minimal technology and only the simplest of tools. Cultural change was gradual, taking place over thousands of years. The great elaboration of Australian and Tasmanian culture was in ritual and social life, also its ancient artistic traditions, which helped maintain the balance between the Aborigines and available food resources in an arid environment. Aboriginal technology developed within Australia over a long period in response to local needs and without the benefit of cultural innovation from outside.

★ ★ ★

Off northern Australia, c. 45,000 years ago or earlier... An outrigger canoe sails quietly before the warm, following wind. A simple watercraft this, its platform is made by fitting a dugout canoe with a basic outrigger, while a second light-hull is lashed to the dugout with plant fibers. The family sits and lies on layers or reeds secured to the underlying timbers. The ancestors had always paddled these canoes, but now a young man steers with a long paddle at the rear. His eyes watch a light skin sail billowing from a short mast, controlled with a fiber line.

Meanwhile, his family gazes at the low-lying coast that lies ahead. As they reach shallow water, they release the sail and let the canoe slide gently aground on the sand. Two youngsters leap ashore with their spears at the ready, alert for hostile folk hiding along a small stream at the head of the sheltered bay. No one appears, for the land is uninhabited. The crew set up camp and light a fire among the trees, making sure they can see for some distance. Next day, they will hunt and forage. Their provisions are running short after several days at sea.

They are among the first human beings to land on this seemingly desolate coast.

FURTHER READING

For a definitive account on the origins of AMH see: John Hoffecker, *Modern Humans: Their African Origin and Global Dispersal* (New York: Columbia University Press, 2017). See also Chris Stringer, *Lone Survivors: How We Came to be the Only Humans on Earth* (New York: Times Books, 2012). San art: David Lewis-Williams, *Image-Makers: The Social Context of a Hunter-Gatherer Ritual* (Cambridge: Cambridge University Press, 2019). Australia: Derek Mulvaney and John Kumminga, *Prehistory of Australia* (Washington, DC: Smithsonian Institution Press, 2019).

MODERN HUMANS IN THE NORTH (C. 50,000 TO 12,000 YEARS AGO)

Niaux Cave, Southwestern France, 13,000 years ago... Fat-fuelled lamps flicker in the darkness as the spirit medium chants. The woman's voice rises and falls with the unfolding narrative. Some of the older people in the great chamber have heard the story before, but the children listen in awe. The superb acoustics of the cavern, 500 meters from the open air, resonate and echo. The audience watches with awe as two columns of black-painted bison seem to move in the flickering light. One bison stands still, as if listening for something. The supernatural power of familiar animals descends on those who hunt them.

About 50,000 years ago—the date is uncertain— anatomically modern humans moved from the Middle East into southeastern Europe, probably in small numbers. They settled in landscapes that were a far cry from the semi-arid landscapes of southwestern Asia. The lands north of the Mediterranean were environments of dramatic seasonal contrasts—short, fairly warm summers, and lengthy winters, often with weeks of sub-zero temperatures.

The last glaciation was in full swing, with huge ice sheets mantling Scandinavia in the north. Mountain glaciers flowed outward from the Alps. Much of Europe between the Atlantic Ocean and the Ural Mountains was open steppe-tundra. River valleys, especially in the west, offered some shelter during the cold months. Here, deep valleys supported lush summer meadows and a mix of open steppe

DOI: 10.4324/9781003177326-4

Figure 4.1 Map showing sites in Chapter 4.

and forest. High cliffs often provided caves and rock shelters warmed by the winter sun. These areas lay astride reindeer migrations in spring and fall, while salmon ran up fast-moving rivers.

INTRODUCING THE CRO-MAGNONS

The newcomers were round-headed folk, first identified from burials at the Cro-Magnon rock shelter near Les Eyzies in southwestern France in 1868. The Cro-Magnon label has caught on and is one we will use here, but be aware that it is just a nickname for members of our species in late Ice Age Europe. Recent genetic analysis indicates that they were black, or certainly very dark-skinned, people, who had arrived in their new homeland during a brief period of more temperate climatic conditions, which did not last long. Europe's late Ice Age climate shifted from one extreme to another irregularly and without notice. This meant that the Cro-Magnons developed elaborate and sophisticated hunting cultures in response.

The first modern humans in Europe survived in this harsh and unpredictable environment, not only because they were expert hunters and foragers, but because they had effective ways of keeping warm outside in sub-zero temperatures. Above all, they were adaptable opportunists, used to cooperating with others, and well aware that diversifying their food quest was key to survival.

Most of the time, the first settlers lived in small groups, living off a wide range of game and stored foods. Most likely, they came together in spring, summer or early fall, when reindeer and other game were abundant, and, in later times, salmon easily taken. This time of year was an important annual occasion when social life was at its most intense. People arranged marriages, conducted initiation rites. They also bartered raw materials like fine-grained toolmaking stone, ceremonial objects, and other commodities with one another. Then, in winter, the people would disperse into small groups based in deep valleys living off local game and stored food.

After the extinction of the Neanderthals by 30,000 years ago, the Cro-Magnons had western and Central Europe to themselves. They developed elaborate and sophisticated societies marked by significant technological innovations. Their cultures also witnessed a flowering of ritual and social life, reflected by one of the earliest art traditions in the world.

Cautious, innovative, and remarkably versatile, diverse Cro-Magnon societies thrived from as early as the mid-40,000s. But their heyday came long after the last Neanderthals had perished, much of it during the so-called Last Glacial Maximum of about 21,000 to 18,000 years ago. Over many generations, modern humans in Europe gradually developed some of the world's first arctic-adapted cultures.

THE FIRST SWISS ARMY KNIFE

The Cro-Magnons used a versatile, but ultimately simple, technology which provided them with all manner of more specialized tools. Like stone toolmakers everywhere, they were selective in their choices of fine-grained rock like chert and flint. They flaked this

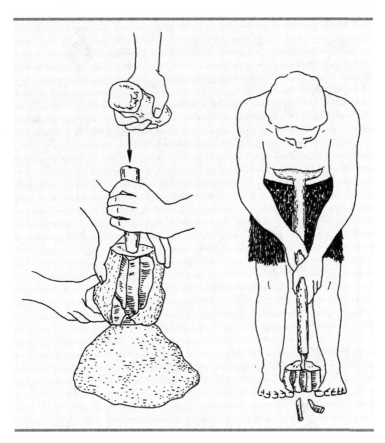

Figure 4.2 Using a punch to manufacture blades. Various tools served to strike off the blade—a hand-held punch (left) or a longer one using one's chest (right). The punch allowed intensive pressure to be applied to a single point on the top of the core and channels the direction of the shock waves.

raw material into carefully shaped nodules. From these cores, they punched off relatively standardized, parallel-sided blades, which served as blanks for a broad array of cutting, scraping, and piercing tools (Figure 4.2).

Think of the Swiss Army knife, which is basically a chassis adorned with hinged blades, which serve as everything from scissors

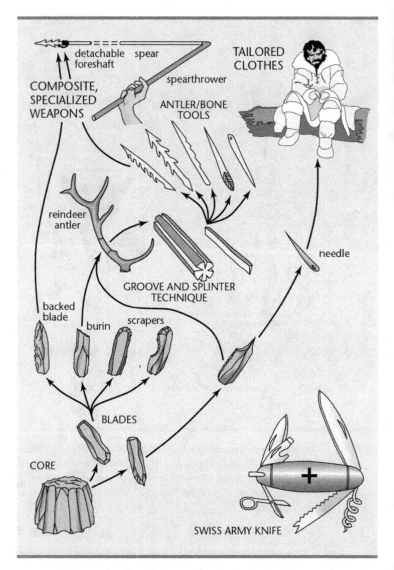

Figure 4.3 The Swiss Army knife effect: blade technology acted like the celebrated Swiss Army Knife, providing blanks for making many specialized tools for working bone and antler.

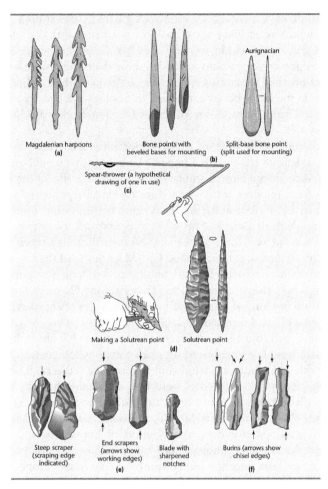

Figure 4.4 Characteristic tools used by modern human groups in western Europe. Antler and bone were of vital importance, especially for harpoons (a) and bone points (b) mounted on wooden shafts. The spear thrower (c) was a hooked shaft, used to propel a spear a longer distance with great accuracy. Stone tools made from blades reached a high degree of sophistication after about 20,000 years ago, with pressure flaked Solutrean points, named after a site in southwestern France. Everyone relied on scrapers (e) for processing skins and other purposes. The chisel-shaped burin (f) was used to groove reindeer antler, bone, and wood for making spear heads.

to toothpicks. Cro-Magnons must have carried cores around with them, which acted like reserve banks of raw material that could be turned into tools within seconds. Butcher a reindeer, there were sharp-edged knives; fashion a wooden spear shaft: there were scrapers and notched spokeshaves; bore fine holes in leather: a flint awl would do the job. Above all, the new technology opened up antler, bone, and ivory, critical raw materials in often treeless landscapes (Figure 4.1).

Two stone tools were of stellar importance. The first was the burin, a delicate chisel with a fine working edge that would groove wood, slice precise lines in animal hides, and, above all, cut the long blanks from reindeer antler needed for making harpoon and spear heads. Many of these antler blanks became barbed points mounted with foreshafts that snapped off when a spear struck its quarry.

The second was the eyed needle. Neanderthals had worn skin garments draped over their bodies. Cro-Magnons used their needles and sinew thread to make tailored, hooded parkas, long pants, underclothing, even tough, warm, boots. They fashioned layered clothing that could be donned or removed as temperatures changed rapidly or when a blizzard threatened. Tailored garments enabled AMHs to hunt and work outside in sub-zero temperatures. Northern hunters could now live year-round on open steppe where arctic winds blew with great force and wind chill factors were staggeringly cold. No one knows when needles were first invented—after all, finding needles is never easy! However, the oldest-known needle comes from the AMH cave site of Sibudu, in South Africa, and dates to 61,000 years ago. Almost certainly, modern humans from Africa brought this useful technology into Europe. However, the picture is fuzzy, not least since the oldest-known needle from Europe dates to 50,000 years ago and comes from the Denisova Cave in Siberia—which was occupied not only by us, but also by the Neanderthals and Denisovians.

Nonetheless, archaeological excavations in caves, rock shelters, and open camps throughout Europe have identified many refinements in modern human technology over the course of 15,000 years. One of these was the spear thrower, a hooked and sometimes weighted device that extended the range and force of a hunting spear to the point that it rivaled the impact of a bow-and-arrow. The celebrated French archaeologist, Henri Breuil, identified four basic cultural traditions during the early 20th century. These culminated in the Magdalenian culture of about 18,000 to 12,000 years ago. Named after the La Madeleine rock shelter on southwestern France's Vezère River, the Magdalenian culture was not only technologically sophisticated, but also concerned with artistic expression and body ornamentation.

THINKING IN PICTURES: CRO-MAGNON ART

By the late Ice Age, people had mastered the ability to think in specific visual images. They would use them as well as chants, recitations, and songs, to share beliefs and ideas. The ancient art traditions of the San of tropical Africa and the Australian Aborigines were wrapped in symbolic meaning, much of which has been lost. The same is true of the rock art found on Sulawesi in Indonesia, dating to before 40,000 years ago (see Figure 3.4 on p. 48).

Ice Age art, like that of many other societies, originally appeared on many perishable materials, from bird feathers to fiber, bark, and leather. Above all, it survived as engravings and paintings on cave and rock shelter walls, also in a dazzling array of engraved portable objects, everything from spear throwers to simple plaques. We've known about these art traditions since 1879, when the Marquis de Sautola, a Spanish nobleman, announced the discovery of magnificent, polychrome bison paintings on the walls of Altamira Cave in northern Spain. The figures, first spotted by his nine-year-old daughter Maria, were so fresh and realistic that experts proclaimed they were modern forgeries. Sautola was vindicated a quarter century later with the discovery of sealed caves with art on their walls in southwest France.

The surviving art occurs over an enormous area, from North Africa to Siberia, with major concentrations in northern Spain, southwestern France, also Central and Eastern Europe. The artists engraved and painted animals, very occasionally humans, and numerous schematic patterns. There are places, too, where human imprints survive on the walls, made by blowing ocher powder onto outstretched hands. Were these attempts to derive power from spiritual animals lurking behind the walls? We do not know.

The same artists engraved antler, bone, and ivory with consummate skill. They created animals in the round, engraved bison with delicate burin strokes, sketching in every detail of eyes, manes, and hair. Some of the earlier artists produced sculptures of women with voluptuous anatomy, commonly known as Venus figurines. Their significance is unknown.

Major art sites like the Grotte de Chauvet, Lascaux and Niaux in France, and Altamira in northern Spain must have been places of unusual religious and symbolic importance. These were major shrines, which may have attracted visitors from a wide area. Other art sites were sacred places known only to a few, like Tuc d'Audoubert in southern France, where two carefully modeled clay bison lie in a dark chamber far from the entrance. There are several locations where the footprints of adults and children are preserved in damp clay, left by people attending ceremonies, perhaps initiation rituals, deep underground.

Cro-Magnon art defies easy interpretation, for its symbolism comes from a world remote from our own. Did the artists create these images as art for art's sake? Or were they symbolically killing their prey before the hunt? Were they drawing out of desperation? Was their art an attempt to impose some control over the world,

Figure 4.5 A bison at Niaux. Note the lance against its flank.

Hemis/Alamy Stock Photo

at a time when habitats were particularly cold and tough? Might that indeed explain the timing of their excessively creative outbursts?

Occasional hand impressions on the cave walls suggest that people derived spiritual power from mythic beasts lurking behind the rock wall—but this is mere speculation. Another allied school of thought argues that the art was highly spiritual and linked with the supernatural through chant and dance in the hands of spirit mediums with perceived supernatural powers. This brilliant art tradition seems to have played an important role in contemporary life, defining the role of humans in a wider supernatural realm. Most likely, the art was a way of transmitting both practical and spiritual knowledge down the generations to the young. They learned of its realities in near darkness and flickering light.

HUNTERS AND FORAGERS ON THE EASTERN STEPPE (C. 45,000 TO 15,000 YEARS AGO)

The more sheltered landscapes of Spain, Southwestern France, and the Mediterranean landscape gave way to vast, open steppe-tundra plains that extended from the Atlantic deep into Siberia, far to the northeast. Seemingly endless, scrub-covered plains extended to the far horizon. Sub-zero temperatures fed by arctic winds lasted for weeks on end, challenging animals and human alike. Ice Age people faced serious challenges—finding sheltered winter camps, creating efficient, tailored clothing for working outside, and storing enough food to last through long winters.

Small bands settled in shallow river valleys that dissected the plains from as early as 45,000 years ago until just before the Last Glacial Maximum about 18,000 years ago. Thereafter, the population rose fairly rapidly, each group centered on a river valley where game was most plentiful and plant foods and fish, could be found during the brief summer months. Here, people constructed dome-shaped winter houses, partially dug into the ground, then walled and roofed with the most convenient raw material—bones from mammoth carcasses. These they fashioned into strong frameworks covered with hides and sod and entered through subterranean tunnels. One estimate calculates that it would have taken some fifteen people about 10 days to build such a dwelling, far more effort than that used for a more temporary encampment.

From as early as 31,000 years ago, for at least 6000 years, dozens of circular dwellings occupied terraces above the Dyje River at Dolní Věstonice, Moravia, marked by concentrations of mammoth bones and simple kilns for baking clay objects. One remarkable grave dating to about 27,600 years ago contains the skeletons of two men between sixteen and eighteen years old, and a woman of about twenty. They lay side by side, their bodies strewn with red ocher. Interestingly, all three of them had impacted wisdom teether. Perhaps they were relatives.

Some of the best preserved sites lie in the shallow river valleys of the East European Plain. Here, people camped on well-drained river terraces close to a permanent water supply and good toolmaking stone as early as 41,000 years ago. The date for AMH settlement here agrees well with data from Western Europe. Twenty-one sites at Kostenki on the Don River were mainly temporary encampments, but there were also more permanent camps, presumably for winter occupation.

Base camps, like Mezhirich on the Ukraine's Dneiper River, which dates to 15,400 years ago, long after the Glacial Maximum, yield large number of bones from beavers and other fur-bearing animals. Such settlements were in use for about six months a year, occupied by about 50 to 60 people, each house belonging to one or two families. During the winter, they lived off meat stored in pits dug into the underlying permafrost, a natural refrigerator. The people relied on seasonal reindeer migrations, and on intensive summer hunting. The same routine endured for thousands of years from before the Last Glacial Maximum until the end of the Ice Age.

NORTHEAST ASIA

Widely separated Late Ice Age groups settled much of the extensive steppe-tundra as far east as Lake Baikal in Siberia. By 25,000 years ago, at least two major hunter-gatherer traditions flourished over wide areas around the lake. Both pursued large animals like mammoth, along with reindeer and smaller animals. Together, these traditions reflect a varied adaptation to an enormous area of Central Asia and southern Siberia from far west of Lake Baikal to the shores of the Pacific Ocean.

Population movements into Siberia originated in many places, not just from the west. As they had elsewhere, the movements resulted from the realities of hunter–gatherer life for people living in small bands. In time, a sparse human population would occupy thousands of square kilometers of steppe-tundra. It was through these natural dynamics of constant movement, extreme social flexibility, and opportunism that people first settled extreme Northeast Asia and passed into the Americas.

We know that northeast Asia supported some human groups as early as 27,000 years ago. The Yana RHS site lies only 140 kilometers from the Arctic Ocean, occupied long before the Last Glacial Maximum of 18,000 years ago. During the Maximum, northeast Siberia was bitterly cold, supporting little vegetation. The few bands that dwelt there must have moved south into warmer landscapes. Human settlement resumed after the coldest millennia, known from sites north and east of Lake Baikal dating to between 20,000 and 15,000 years ago. Many were associated by a cultural tradition called Dyuktai, widespread after 18,000 years ago, identified by distinctive stone spear points.

Another important technological innovation originated in temperate Asia, perhaps in areas like the Gobi Desert and Mongolia, where people hunted over enormous distances. They developed a stone technology of small "microblades" that were easily portable and readily mounted as spearheads. Such toolkits, highly effective against caribou and other animals, spread into the harsh landscapes of northeast Siberia. And from there, the same technology passed over the dry land of the Bering Strait into Alaska, together with stone spear points that became important in later millennia.

THE BERINGIAN STANDSTILL (25,000 AND 11,500 YEARS AGO)

Most archaeologists believe that the first inhabitants of the Americas arrived there by way of the Bering land bridge. They walked to Alaska, for the low sea levels of the last glaciation had exposed a low-lying, windy, land mass. This forms the central part of an Ice Age land, which geologists have named Beringia.

Beringia was seemingly inhospitable. Frigid winds swept across the shallow valleys that dissected the steppe-tundra with its cold winters. The amount of exposed land varied considerably, reducing the land bridge to a narrow isthmus during the warmer millennia before the Late Glacial Maximum. Between 25,000 and 11,500 years ago, sea levels dropped with a renewed decline in temperature. Dry land extended from Asia to Alaska, northward into the Arctic Ocean and as far as the Aleutian Islands. Thanks to core borings, we know that the land bridge supported a diverse array of habitats. Surprisingly, parts of it were more hospitable than one might assume.

Geneticists have provisionally timed the split between people who settled in Siberia and those in North America to between 24,900 and 18,400 years ago. It seems likely that there was a single migration eastward onto the land bridge as the Last Glacial Maximum intensified, then receded.

Now the plot thickens. Core borings from the southeastern portions of the land bridge reveal reduced topography and a relatively high level of plant productivity, owing to the proximity of the North Pacific Ocean. This area may have been a unique habitat for people living in southern Beringia. Owing to the Pacific, temperature decline during the Last Glacial Maximum was smaller than that for the other parts of the Northern Hemisphere. Much of the land bridge may have been inhospitable, but the southeast may have been a refuge. This was where the ancestors of the first Americans thrived during the coldest millennia.

This theory, known as the Beringian Standstill Hypothesis, is a tentative explanation for a critical moment in first settlement. Perhaps 8000 to 10,000 people lived over a large area of Beringia. Then, as temperatures warmed and sea levels gradually rose after 15,000 years ago, they moved from Beringia onto higher ground to the east. Perhaps the first visits were seasonal and confined to the summer months, with the refuge beckoning a return in winter. As the North American ice sheets began a retreat after 17,000 years ago, the isolation of Beringia's people ended, especially as coastal areas to the south opened up.

MOVING INTO NORTH AMERICA
(C. 15,000 YEARS AGO AND LATER)

The first settlement of the Americas has generated intense controversy for over a century. After all these years, there is limited consensus. But almost everyone agrees that neither Neanderthals nor Denisovans ever settled in the Americas. The first Americans were *Homo sapiens*.

But when did they cross into North America? There is broad agreement that first settlement took place during warming after the Last Glacial Maximum. This narrows the time frame to sometime between 18,000 and 15,000 years ago. Most experts tend to favor a date around 15,000 to 16,000 years ago.

For more than a century, anthropologists have drawn attention to the biological similarities between Siberians and Native North Americans. Native American teeth have a pattern of dental features that link them to northern Asian populations. Our old friend mtDNA suggests that all Native Americans are descended ultimately from a somewhat diverse group of Asians from eastern Siberia and Beringia.

As temperatures warmed, a tiny human population spread over the vast Alaskan landscape, developing distinctive cultures over very long periods of time. At the Swan Point site in the Tenana River watershed, numerous hearths, radiocarbon dated to about 14,200 years ago, document an occupation of Dyuktai people from western Beringia. Some temporary encampments have also survived on well-drained ridges in the Nenana Valley southeast of Fairbanks and nearby. The camps overlook marshy lowlands where game would have grazed in summer. The radiocarbon dates for the sites are around 13,000 to 11,500 years ago.

As temperatures warmed significantly, dozens of small population movements brought people into the hitherto deserted lands, people grouped into a little known Northern Paleo-Indian tradition. This is thought of as the northern equivalent of Paleo-Indian traditions further south, as described below. (The generic term Paleo-Indian refers to early hunter-gatherer societies in the Americas.) Some of these people, perhaps numbering only dozens, were the first to move southward, either by land or sea, into the temperate landscapes that lay south of the great North American ice sheets.

Whether ancestral Native Americans moved southward through the interior or along the Pacific Coast is an unresolved question. With good reason, too, given the demanding territory for the necessary fieldwork. For generations, experts assumed that the first settlers arrived in the American heartland by land. They based their argument on the great ice sheets of the last glaciation that fused into a huge frozen wilderness before 18,000 years ago. Then warming began and the ice sheets parted, leaving an ice-free corridor to the south.

The corridor theory became a kind of mental 'freeway' that brought Native Americans southward at a time when no one had surveyed its hypothetical pathway. Did such a freeway actually exist? Intensive surveys now date thawing beginning in the north of the corridor route around 19,000 years ago, with much exposed landscape elsewhere by 15,000, and around the southern end by 13,000 BP. There may not have been a corridor, but there were certainly viable, if demanding, routes to the south soon after first settlement in the north.

Or did the earliest migrants travel southward through ice-free coastal areas along the Alaskan and British Columbian coasts? Unfortunately, many of their camps and more permanent settlements are deep below modern sea levels. Two sites in Haida Gwaii, off the coast of British Columbia date to about 12,800 years ago, but there must have been earlier occupations. Extensive tracts of open tundra along the then-exposed continental shelf would have attracted hunters from the interior. They would also have begun fishing and sea mammal hunting, major occupations of their descendants. Like the interior, the coast route was viable, if challenging. At this point, we can only assume that both routes were usable, but not necessarily by simple means.

Whatever the details of initial settlement, both genetics, and a growing number of dated DNA samples, hint at rapid population growth and dispersal of humans throughout the Americas between 14,500 and 13,000 years ago. Certainly, people were living on the coast of South America by 14,000 years ago, and were visiting Santa Rosa Island off Southern California by 13,000 BP.

A FAINT SIGNATURE OF EARLY SETTLEMENT (?C. 14,000 YEARS AGO AND LATER)

The first Native Americans south of the ice sheets are practically invisible except for a handful of sites that date to before 12,000 years ago. Most of what we know about them comes from scatters of stone tools, an archaeological signature typical of highly mobile, hunter-gatherers with small, portable toolkits.

The initial moves into new, unoccupied lands found people moving widely and far to the south. Computer modeling suggests that hunter-gatherer populations could have traversed the Americas within about 2000 years from first arrival. This estimate assumes that the settlers took paths that were the least arduous, those most likely to yield food and toolmaking materials. The actual process of settlement may have involved bands 'leap-frogging' as they split into new territories, often a long distance away. This may be why very early sites are widely spaced over the continent.

And spaced they are: some people visited the Paisley Five Mile site in Oregon's Cascade Mountains and left feces behind them that date to around 14,290 years ago. The lowest levels of the long-inhabited Meadowcroft rock shelter in Pennsylvania were occupied as early as 14,500 years ago. The Cactus Hill sand dune in Virginia has a hearth and projectile points said to date as early as 15,000 to 16,600 years BP. In northeastern Florida, the Page-Ladson site saw a group of hunters kill and butcher a mastodon 14,550 years ago. And so the evidence of early settlement in North America slowly accumulates for a highly scattered human population before 14,000 years ago.

For years, virtually everyone assumed that the well-known Clovis people of 13,050 to 12,800 years ago, with their distinctive spear points, were the first Americans. Wrong! We now know that there were earlier settlers, about whom we still know very little. The Clovis people appeared suddenly and spread widely over the Great Plains and eastern North America. Like other early Native American societies, they were highly mobile, versatile hunter-gatherers, who could kill animals of all sizes and also depended on plant foods, and fish. The Clovis population was sparse and often relied on unpredictable environments for food. This meant that social contacts and intelligence gathered over long distances were of great importance. The Paleo-Indian population rose over many generations. By 10,500 years ago, well-defined regional projectile forms reflected a much greater variety of adaptations to local environments as Native American life moved in new directions.

Further south in the Americas, data on first settlement is still elusive. Chiquihuite Cave in Central Mexico is said to have human occupation dated to as early as 25,000 to 32,000 years ago. However, questions have been raised about the stone tools found there and the context and opinion remains divided on the subject. Genetics suggest that there were multiple migrations from the north into South America, the first thought to be around 14,000 years ago. There are traces of human settlement at Huaca Prieta on the Peruvian coast by that date. Far to the south in southern Chile, the Monte Verde site dates to between 13,800 and 14,000 years ago. The excavator, Tom Dillehay, uncovered two rows of skin-covered rectangular houses joined by connecting walls. The inhabitants occupied this long-term camp site near a forest, where plant foods were abundant and a major element in the diet, which also included game.

The earliest known settlements are widely scattered, one in Brazil dating to 12,700 to 11,700. The Cuncaicha rock shelter in the Andean highlands was occupied around 12,400 years ago, at the same time as Swan Point in distant Alaska. Future research is bound to fill in the picture of a complex process of first settlement.

With the first settlement of the Americas sometime between 16,000 and 15,000 years ago, *Homo sapiens* had now colonized the world. This was also the time when natural global warming transformed the late Ice Age world beyond recognition and new chapters in the human past brought far more complex human societies onto the stage.

★ ★ ★

North American Great Basin, early fall, 12,000 years ago... Two Paleo-Indian bands have brought fiber nets with them. They camp in a familiar rock shelter close to a spring, where rabbits forage in the sagebrush. In the cool of morning, men and women spread out their nets to form a large rectangle. The women light a fire close to an edge of the net. When it is well alight, the men walk in a line inside the net, driving the rabbits before them. Some are trapped in the head-sized mesh, but most panic and crowd to the end of the rectangle. Wooden clubs and spears come into play. Both men and women beat the undergrowth to drive out hiding animals. Women and children gather up the carcasses and process them as the men reset the enclosure and repeat the process again and again. By the end of the day, dozens of rabbit skins and carcasses hang on racks to dry. The hunt has yielded enough pelts to make enough warm blankets for the coming winter.

FURTHER READING

A definitive general work, already cited in Chapter 3: John Hoffecker, *Modern Humans: Their African Origin and Global Dispersal* (New York: Columbia University Press, 2017). Late Ice Age settlement in Europe: Brian Fagan, *Cro-Magnon: How the Ice Age Gave Birth to the First Modern Humans* (New York: Bloomsbury Press, 2010). Late Ice Age art: Paul Bahn, *Images of the Ice Age* (Oxford: Oxford University Press, 2016). Eurasia: John Hoffecker, *A Prehistory of the North* (New Brunswick: Rutgers University Press, 2005). See also his *Desolate Landscapes* (New Brunswick: Rutgers University Press, 2002). Beringia: John Hoffecker and Scott Elias, *Human Ecology of Beringia* (New York: Columbia University Press, 2007. The Americas: Brian Fagan, *Ancient North America: The Archaeology of a Continent*, 5th ed. (London: Thames & Hudson, 2019).

5

AFTER THE ICE (C. 15,000 YEARS AGO AND LATER)

The Great Basin, western United States, Fall, c. 2500 BCE... The men have carefully removed their prized feather decoys and snares from the storage pit in the floor of Hogup Cave. They clean the bone tubes which they use as snorkels. Long before dawn, they crouch in the reeds around the lake, watching the sleeping waterfowl in deeper water. A few of the hunters slip quietly underwater with bird decoys on their heads. They leave not a ripple, moving silently toward the sleeping birds, breathing through the bone tubes. Suddenly, a duck vanishes below the surface, grabbed by the neck, its neck wrung in seconds. The still twitching prey is pushed quickly into a netting bag. The hunter is not alone. Decoys, seemingly identical to living birds, move quietly among the ducks, thinning them one by one.

A WARMING WORLD (AFTER 16,000 YEARS AGO)

By 16,000 years ago, the world's northern ice sheets were in full retreat across Britain, Scandinavia, and North America. Sea levels were rising from their global low around 90 meters below modern levels. Rising sea water gradually inundated the great continental shelf and the now-sunken landmasses of Sunda and Sahul off Southeast Asia. The Bering Land Bridge was shrinking and

DOI: 10.4324/9781003177326-5

Britain was becoming an island as Doggerland vanished beneath the North Sea.

The warming climate oscillated between irregular cycles of colder and warmer cycles. Extensive birch, pine, and poplar forests had replaced open steppe over much of Britain, northern Germany and Scandinavia. All these climatic changes were rapid by geological standards. The warming brought with it earlier springs and nesting seasons, less snowfall, and better grazing for beasts such as wild horses and bison. By 14,000 years ago, small groups of people had settled across the Americas. Everywhere, they still lived in the same basic way as their ancestors and assumed that their descendants would have the same kind of existence. In the longer term, the changes to human life were profound, especially in Europe and more northern lands. Fortunately, the flexibility of hunter-gatherer life enabled bands to adapt effortlessly to a changed world, even if there were major changes in the quest for food.

Late Ice Age people in Central and Western Europe followed their accustomed prey, like reindeer, northward, seeking more open country and cooler temperatures. So did hunting bands, who ambushed migrating reindeer by shallow northern lakes. As temperatures continued to rise, Northwestern Europe changed profoundly. The North Sea was a low-lying, marshy expanse (Figure 5.1). The Rhine, the Seine, and the Thames rivers flowed into a wide estuary that is now the English Channel. By 11,000 years ago, human settlement was shifting northward into a dynamic, rapidly changing world of shallow estuaries, mudflats and sand banks with staggering biodiversity. Many groups settled on the shore of a northern lake that became the Baltic Sea. Here, bird life, fish, and mollusks soon became staples of coastal and lakeside life. Some bands could remain at one location for months on end.

Unfortunately, most settlements of the day are below modern sea levels. Other bands settled on higher ground. One group repeatedly visited the shores of a glacial lake at Star Carr in northeastern England for about three centuries around 10,500 years ago. They settled on slightly higher ground and hunted deer in spring and early summer in the nearby birch woods. On several occasions, they burned the reeds that fronted the water to get a better view and easier launching for their dugout canoes. Only a fragmentary paddle now survives from their watercraft.

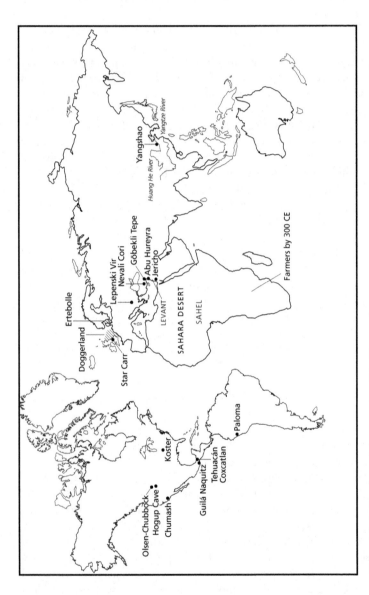

Figure 5.1 Archaeological sites mentioned in Chapter 5.

COASTAL AND INLAND PEOPLE IN EUROPE (C. 9000 TO 3000 BCE)

Dugout canoes, antler-headed fishing spears, nets, and fish traps—all evidence that the peoples who settled along Baltic coasts spent much of their lives afloat or wading in shallow water. Their now-water-logged settlements have yielded rich hauls of artifacts that rarely survive underground. We know that their most important weapons were the barbed fish spear, often with double or triple heads and the bow-and arrow. They used arrows tipped with razor-sharp microliths (tiny blades), which served as points or barbed arrows (Figure 5.2). The

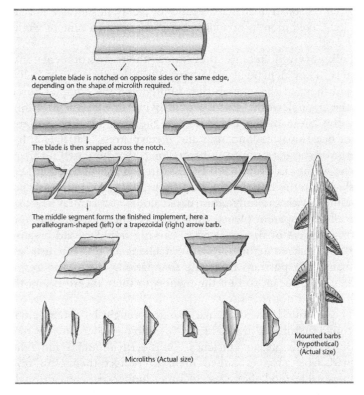

Figure 5.2 Microliths. Stages in manufacturing a microlith. A small arrow barb or similar implement made by notching a blade and snapping off its base after the implement is formed.

hunters became expert at shooting birds on the wing with arrows, clubbing them when they fell to ground. So abundant were food supplies that populations rose steadily, crowded into ever more intensively exploited hunting territories. Territories shrank; competition for fishing ground and shellfish intensified. By 7000 BCE, the antagonism sometimes erupted into violence, as reflected by casualties in the local cemeteries.

Over much of Europe, people lived in a landscape of dense woodland. Most bands were no more than few families, who hunted forest game like deer and the occasional bear or wild ox. Above all, they subsisted off a wide variety of tubers and nuts, fruit and edible grasses. The forest was a different environment, but the realities of survival remained unchanged—times of plenty in summer and fall, yet long, cold months of winter and spring; often a time of famine and death.

Folk survived because they knew their environments intimately. They depended on others. Their intricate ritual beliefs linked them to the animals they hunted and the complex forces of the natural world. Even people living in pleasant locations, like the banks of the Iron Gates of the river Danube, suffered from occasional malnutrition and dietary stress. Yet they fished the great sturgeon, up to 9 meters long, that migrated upstream in the spring. In about 6300 BCE, sturgeon fishers dwelt at Lepenski Vir in the heart of the Iron Gates, living in trapeze-shaped dwellings with carefully constructed floors and central hearths.[1] For all the apparent plenty, they were careful to honor the life-giving powers of the great river, carving boulders and creating portraits that sometimes resembled elements of both fish and humans. The portraits lie in the foundations of their houses, as if they were meant to link the owners to their ancestors and the river at their doorsteps.

The profound environmental changes brought by natural global warming meant that people began to exploit a wider range of food resources with greater efficiency. Short-term droughts and other unpredictable changes caused them to protect themselves from unforeseeable food shortages. In time, hunter-gatherers throughout Europe underwent profound adaptation, and, in some areas, acquired greater social complexity.

Limited complexity among hunter-gather societies was already present in some late Ice Age societies, notably the Magdalenians of southwest France and northern Spain. With post-Ice Age warming, social complexity became most common in areas where freshwater or marine fish, shellfish, or sea mammals were abundant. In northern Europe, Baltic shores witnessed a population explosion and increased social complexity, reflected in the Ertebolle culture, which appeared around 4500 BCE, centered on coastal Denmark and Sweden.

ERTEBOLLE CULTURE (C. 4500 TO AFTER 3000 BCE)

Their predecessors had been more mobile, but Ertebolle communities tended to stay at one location for generations. Most of their fishing, targeting coastal species, took place over the summer months. They were experts at fishing with stationary traps, set in places with strong currents like river mouths or narrow inlets. Some traps were large-scale, permanent structures anchored with hazelwood stakes. The fishers also used bone books and barbed, multipronged spears, but the varied catch almost all came from traps. They took eels in large numbers with bottle-shaped snares. During the cold months, they relied heavily on dried and carefully stored fish and nuts, and enormous numbers of mollusks. The empty shells accumulated in huge middens are valuable archives for archaeologists. There were fewer Ertebolle settlements inland, most lie near lakes where pike and perch could be taken in vegetated water with soft beds. Low-tech Ertebolle fishing methods were so effective that they remained in use until the Industrial Revolution.

Ertebolle populations rose steadily until about 4000 BCE, when territories became more constrained and permanent settlement more commonplace. Survival in any Ertebolle territory required careful timing, some seasonal movement, and constant intelligence about inshore fish movements acquired from the shore and by canoe. This intricate knowledge passed from generation to generation by example, also by oral recitation and chants, and through rituals that honored supernatural beings and the ancestors, who were the intermediaries to the supernatural realm.

The Baltic fishers were unusual in their strong focus on fish and mollusks. But this is no surprise, given the cold climate, which tended to inhibit agriculture in much of Scandinavia until after 3000 BCE (see Chapter 6).

SOUTHWEST ASIA AFTER THE ICE AGE (C. 15,000 YEARS AGO TO 8,500 BCE)

Fifteen thousand years ago, small and highly mobile hunter-gatherer bands inhabited a variety of environments in what is often called the Levant (The eastern Mediterranean coast and inland). Collectively, these people are known as the Kebaran, their sites remarkable for thousands of small geometric microliths, used for hunting not only in wooded landscapes, but in the steppe and in the Negev and Sinai deserts. They placed a high premium on mobility, essential in semi-arid environments, which resulted in great variation in their toolkits. In some areas, the people dispersed to highlands in summer, moving into caves and rock shelters near lowland lakes in the winter. It seems that hunting was more important than plant foods, for they lacked the numerous grinders and pounders discovered in late settlements, which relied more heavily on wild grasses.

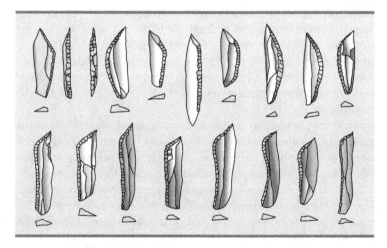

Figure 5.3 Geometric Kebaran microliths. The Kebarans manufactured these in large numbers to serve as arrow barbs.

THE NATUFIANS (C. 11,000 TO 8500 BCE)

The Kebarans had been accomplished hunters, but the Natufians intensified the chase. They targeted migrating gazelle (small, desert antelopes) in spring and fall, and relied heavily on stored harvests of acorns, almonds and pistachios, also wild grasses. The most important settlements became much larger, with an average area of about 700 square meters. Larger Natufian sites lay near to the boundaries between the coastal plains and the uplands, and close to outcrops of good toolmaking stone. Such settlements enabled the Natufians to exploit spring cereal crops, fall nut harvests, and the game that thrived in the oak woodlands. Unlike their mobile predecessors, they enjoyed many months of plentiful food.

New, more complex social orders came into being in a landscape that was becoming increasingly populated. Issues like spacing between settlements and territorial boundaries may have become more important. The dead were buried in graves within some settlements, which also suggests a more permanent attachment to specific communities and locations—to ancestral lands. There are also signs of social ranking, marked by more elaborate grave goods in some burials. Perhaps social status based on kin association developed in response for a need to be able to redistribute valuable food supplies and to maintain order within larger sedentary communities. All of these changes were a preadaptation to the major changes on the horizon.

MEANWHILE, IN THE AMERICAS ... AFTER 9500 BCE)

The end of the cold, Younger Dryas episode, described in Chapter 6, ended in about 9500 BCE. The warming that followed brought dramatic changes in rainfall patterns, sea levels, and vegetation throughout North America. Temperate zones spread northward as continental shelves vanished. Greater environmental diversity challenged Paleo-Indian societies living in isolated bands with usually only sporadic contacts with neighbors. Their varied responses and remarkable opportunism laid the foundations for the great diversity of later Native American societies (Figure 5.4).

The most significant long-term climatic change was towards greater aridity, especially in the west. Those living there responded by broadening the food quest. They had inherited an impressive

Figure 5.4 Early archaeological sites in the Americas, including possible settlement routes.

knowledge of local environments from their ancestors and they now paid closer attention to smaller animals, also to fish and mollusks, and, above all, to plant foods of all kinds. The successors of the first Americans adapted to a remarkable variety of environments from deserts and semi-arid landscapes to fertile river floodplains and coast-lines, both with wide arrays of foods close to hand, and, of course, to arctic landscapes in the far north. However, life was never easy, even in the most food plentiful environments. Everyone diversified their diets and adopted conservative hunting and foraging strategies in order to survive.

THE PLAINS: AFTER CLOVIS (12,800 YEARS AGO TO THE 16TH CENTURY CE)

On the Plains, the successors of the Clovis people thrived on huge tracts of grassland that extended from the frontiers of Alaska to the shores of the Gulf of Mexico. This was the "great bison belt", where the beasts became short grass eaters, as this type of grassland spread during and after the Younger Dryas. Bison populations were highly mobile, so Plains people continued to take a broad range of other prey such as deer, pronghorn antelope and smaller animals including rodents.

Mass bison drives on foot were rare, but dramatic occurrences. At Folsom, New Mexico, a group of hunters killed thirty-two members of a cow-calf herd by working a steep-sided arroyo. They then carried off the rib racks, leaving the butchered carcasses in the gully, where they were covered by wind-blown sand. Drives like this on any scale required careful advance planning, for it is only possible to drive a herd a short distance before they panic and scatter. Such hunts required the cooperation of several bands. The hunters influenced the movements of their quarry for days, moving them in the right direction. Once everything was in place, they would steer the stampeding herd with decoys, even waving skins at the beasts. The sheer mass and weight of the galloping herd would force their descent into the narrow defile and to their deaths.

There are numerous kill sites, each the result of a dramatic event. One of the best known hunts occurred in 7400 BCE at Olsen-Chubbock near Kit Carson, Colorado. Archaeologist Joe Ben Wheat excavated 100 male and 80 female bison carcasses crammed into a buried arroyo. Around 50 percent were adult beasts, the remainder younger. Wheat was even able to estimate the direction of the wind on the day of the hunt, for the bison were driven downwind. He reconstructed the efficient butchery that followed, first, the more accessible beasts, then those jammed into the arroyo. Each beast was rolled onto its belly. The butchers cut the skin along the back and stripped it from the sides to serve as a sort of table for the butchered meat. They then removed the forelimbs, working at high speed. Using Blackfoot Indian examples, Wheat estimated that the process unfolded like the modern assembly line. He estimated that ten people would take about three days to dismember the 140 complete and partially accessible carcasses. The yields were enormous. The hunters acquired some 26,635 kilograms of fresh meat, also 350 kilograms of marrow grease and 2,285 kilograms of tallow.

Olsen–Chubbock and other sites offer dramatic portraits of ancient Plains bison hunts, but such mass drives were rare events. Broad-spectrum hunting and foraging continued unabated, with individual groups adapting to different kinds of hunting and foraging including in woodlands and mountain foothills. We know of these various cultural traditions from a confusing variety of stone projectile points, but we lack many details of their lives, except for knowledge of the intensification of bison hunting that included the construction of corrals to pen the stampeding beasts used during major drives. The rhythm of Plains life continued almost unchanged until the Spanish introduced the horse in the late 16th century.

THE WESTERN INTERIOR (C. 10,000 BCE TO MODERN TIMES)

Dry caves and rock shelters in the arid landscapes of the western interior chronicle a way of life that changed little over thousands of years. Every group that lived in these arid landscapes survived by anchoring itself to reliable water supplies and by diversifying their food quest. The most abundant foods lay by major lakes and rivers, and in wetland areas. As the climate warmed and became drier, so local environmental variability increased, creating cultural variation between different groups. But, for all these local differences, everything depended on carefully planned mobility, detailed ecological knowledge, and consummate flexibility. Toolkits and technology remained simple and portable. Simple implements allowed people to process a broad range of seeds, plants and tubers with minimal technology, the most important tools being flat grinding stones and mullers, and coiled baskets.

Most people lived in small groups of fellow kin, which moved depending on the availability of seasonal food at widely separated locations. People harvested wild grasses by tapping the seeds into baskets or gathering them by hand. Hardwood digging sticks allowed them to harvest root crops like yampa and other tubers. Berries, piñon nuts, and acorns were valuable foods, gathered by women in chest baskets. Both the latter are rich in protein, while acorns have a high fat content. Each could be readily stored, so the early fall was a busy time.

Riverbanks, marshes, and lakes, also locations near wetlands, were magnets for human settlement over many generations. Hogup Cave in Utah lies near wetlands and was visited regularly from about 7840 BCE for thousands of years. The dry layers have preserved all manner of perishable artifacts, including nets, sandals, even fragments of fur blankets. The inhabitants ate rabbits caught with nets and other small animals, hunted deer and wild sheep, and took some fish.

The art of survival depended on exploiting an edible landscape of extreme aridity. The people moved constantly from lower to higher elevations, following harvest seasons, appearing at once by temporary lakes when rare rain fell. Adjustments in group size and composition, and technological innovations, like the bow-and-arrow in 500 CE, served as adaptations to changing circumstances. Above all, so did increasingly intensive exploitation of a broad range of foods.

BACK AT THE COAST

One of the pathways for first settlement was the Pacific Coast, where fish, mollusks, and sea mammals abounded. No one knows when serious maritime exploitation began, but we know that by 6000 BCE some groups were relying heavily on salmon runs and inshore herring fisheries. Salmon runs provided enormous numbers of fish, more than could be dried or salted. The runs varied in distribution and quantity each year, but, by 3000 BCE or so, increasingly intensive manipulation of the salmon runs produced food surpluses not only to feed people, but also to satisfy social and ideological needs. By then, cedar forests abounded along the Northwest Coast, which provided firewood for large-scale fish smoking and the raw materials for cedar-planked houses, used as dwellings and for food storage.

Salmon and halibut were of paramount importance in the coastal diet, so much so that carbon isotopes reveal an almost total dependence on maritime foods. Coastal society became more complex. Village-to-village trade routes carried obsidian from as far afield as eastern Oregon and near Juneau, Alaska. These exchange networks, and others handling different commodities, spread ideas and culture traits over wide areas. This was when an emphasis on status and wealth came to the forefront, reflected in elaborate ceremonials reflected in new art traditions.

Meanwhile, fishing became ever more intensive, with the fishers using large, cedar dugout canoes to fish further offshore. Fishing technology included not only spears and harpoons, but all manner of traps, often associated with weirs, and composite lethal fishing hooks. Each group wrestled with the problems of managing and redistributing increasingly large food surpluses, and social rank and its accompanying regalia such as body ornaments assumed ever greater importance as reflected in ceremonial feasts that preceded the elaborate potlatches of more recent times. By 500 CE, all the basic elements of more complex, later Northwestern societies were in place.

The northwest coast was no placid landscape inhabited by peaceful and prosperous tribal groups. This was an intensely competitive, sometimes violent world, where chiefs pursued power, prestige, and wealth through trade in prosaic commodities such as dried flesh and gifts of ceremonial regalia with single-minded intensity. Factionalism, violent quarrels, and aggressive inter-group diplomacy were routine.

COASTAL PEOPLE: THE CHUMASH AND OTHERS
(C. 6000 BCE TO HISTORICAL TIMES)

Further south, rocky and mountainous coastal habitats supported sparse hunter-gatherer populations for thousands of years. They subsisted on a mix of plant foods, sea mammals, mollusks, and fish, moving constantly between seasonal food sources. To the south, San Francisco Bay with its two converging river systems became inundated by rising sea levels, so much so that marshes and wetlands provided a remarkable array of animal and plant life. As the marsh-lands grew, so did the human population. As the marshlands expanded, so bands settled on mounds surrounded by muddy flats at low tide. Some mounds, especially those near productive oyster and clam beds and productive shallow water fisheries, became major base camps.

Population densities increased here and inland along major rivers. But the coastal population of much of Central and Southern California remained low for millennia. Here, people owed much to earlier Paleo-Indian culture, with the addition of milling stones and pounders for processing plant foods.

The population of the Santa Barbara Channel increased around 6000 BCE, but especially after people focused on harvesting acorns. Maritime productivity also rose as kelp beds with their rich fisheries reappeared close offshore. Over many centuries, exploitation of acorns and marine resources intensified dramatically. This coincided with an elaboration of technology, art, and social institutions in what was always a high risk environment. Severe drought cycles, and short-term fluctuations in rainfall and sea water temperatures, could descend at any time. Between 1000 BCE and 1000 CE, coastal Chumash people depended ever more heavily on the ocean. They took deep water fish from planked canoes known in later times as *tomols*.

Increased population densities, more complex political rivalries, and an increasingly elaborate ceremonial life: major Chumash villages now housed as many as 1000 people, each headed by a hereditary chief (*wot*), who served as a war leader and patron of ceremonial village feasts. Chumash art is justly famous for its abstract depictions of the sun, stars, human beings, also birds, fish, and reptiles. Shamans and specialists served as the artists for a tradition that involved a profound knowledge of the heavenly bodies.

The increasing complexity of Chumash coastal populations may have resulted not from plentiful food supplies as severe drought brought inland groups to the more plentifully endowed coast in search of food. There were complex political issues to resolve, such as the maintenance of territorial boundaries while also regulating food supplies and trade. Whatever the strategies that came into play, Chumash societies flourished in the Santa Barbara Channel region for more than 3000 years, and up until European contact during the 16th century CE and beyond.

There is a tendency to think of the West Coast as a sort of Garden of Eden, blessed with benign climatic conditions and bountiful foods. Reality was something very different. The climate was unpredictable: long, irregular drought cycles could create constant food shortages. This was no Garden of Eden, but a diverse landscape that challenged survival.

THE WOODLANDS OF THE EAST (C. 8000 TO 2000 BCE)

Eastern woodlands societies flourished from the Great Lakes and the St. Lawrence Valley in the north to the Gulf of Mexico and from the Atlantic Ocean to the Mississippi in the west. This huge region supported a broad diversity of hunter-gatherer societies. Most lived off forest animals such as deer, and, increasingly over the millennia, on plant foods and nut harvests. People adapted with varying success to a wide variety of local environments. Populations rose significantly in favored locations like river valley floors, lakesides, and coastal estuaries. By 4000 BCE or so, the overall population was such that territories became more restricted and much reduced. This was one of the reasons why plant foods and nut harvests became more important. People exploited food resources more productively, but the basic way of life remained virtually unchanged throughout most of the Holocene.

Between about 4500 and 4000 BCE, many midwestern and southeastern rivers stabilized and accumulated silt in their floodplains as a result of more stationary sea levels. Shallow water and more sluggish rivers provided abundant fish and mollusks. These became major components in the diet, so that many groups adopted more sedentary lifeways in parts of the eastern woodlands. Whether this was the result of an opportunistic response to seasonally abundant foods or to increased population densities, causing people to turn to alternative food sources, is unknown.

We know, however, that some favored locations remained in use for most of, if not all, the year. The Koster site in the Illinois River Valley was visited by nearby groups at least as early as 8500 BCE, a substantial settlement flourishing there between 5600 and 5000 BCE. The inhabitants lived in pole and branch houses, which they occupied most of the year. Between 3900 and 2800 BCE, permanent settlements of round huts thrived at Koster. Their owners netted large numbers of river fish, as much as 270 kilograms per 0.4 hectare. They also relied heavily on nut harvests and waterfowl. The Illinois River lies on the Mississippi flyway, a migration route used by millions of waterfowl flying to and from their Canadian breeding grounds each spring and fall. Hundreds of ducks and geese slept on the water, so hunters caught them with bows and arrows or by deftly thrown light nets.

Koster was but one of dozens of such settlements of different sizes, many of which served as regular base camps, from which people moved to exploit nut harvests and other seasonal foods. At the same time, isolation, characteristic of earlier times, broke down, replaced by more complex social and political relationships. There was also a new concern with relationships between natural and supernatural realms, with the commemoration of ancestors and the construction of mounds and earthworks to celebrate them, described more fully in Chapter 7. Formal gift-giving and kin ties between powerful individuals were to play a major role in eastern woodland societies of later times.

★★★

Northern California foothills, fall 1500 BCE... The band has watched the ripening acorns for days, waiting for the moment they're ready for harvest. Timing is critical. Too late, and the ripe nuts will fall into the mouths of waiting deer. The people have camped by the oaks for days, while the men hunted the deer. The day of the harvest arrives. Everyone is up at dawn, stripping a large tree or two smaller ones of their ripe acorns all in a day's work. While the men climb the trees, the women and children load the harvest into baskets and haul them laboriously back to camp. Now the real work begins. The mortars are dug up having been buried after the previous year's harvest. Meanwhile, others crack the shells with hammer stones, then inspect and winnow them, finally pounding them into meal. The thumping is an art, requiring hours of pounding in several shapes and grades of depression to achieve a fine-grain acorn meal. But the work has barely begun: the pounded acorns are spread in a porous depression in the ground, then leached with water for two to six hours to eliminate toxins. The nuts, or their processed meal, will either be used within a short time, or more likely carried back to the winter base camp. There the women heft the unused nuts into thatched granaries, waterproofed with bark. A large granary could feed six people for an entire year.

FURTHER READING

For a truly global account of what happened after the Ice Age, see Steven Mithen, *After the Ice: A Global Human History, 20,000 to 5000 BC* (Cambridge, MA: Harvard University Press, 2006); Ofer Bar-Yosef and François R. Valla, *Natufian Foragers in the Levant Terminal Pleistocene* (New York: Berghahn Books, 2013). Scholarly essays on the Natufian. Lepenski Vir: Geoff Bailey and Penny Spikins (eds.), *Mesolithic Europe* (Cambridge: Cambridge University Press, 2008). The essay in this book by Clive Bonsall on the Mesolithic of the Iron Gates describes the site (pp. 238–79). Ertebolle: Inge Bodker Enghoff, "Fishing in Denmark during the Ertebolle Period," *International Journal of Osteoarchaeology* 4 (1994): 65–96. North America: Brian Fagan, *Ancient North America: The Archaeology of a Continent.* 5th ed. (London: Thames & Hudson, 2019).

NOTE

1 From here on, we use BCE/CE for dates after 10,000 BCE.

6

FARMERS AND HERDERS (C. 10,000 BCE AND LATER)

Abu Hureyra, Syria, fall, 8000 BCE. Scrape, scrape… the sound embraces the growing settlement close to the Euphrates River. Soon after dawn, the monotonous routine begins and continues all day. Each woman kneels over her quern with a saddle-shaped grindstone, outside a small dwelling sunk partially into the ground. Their bodies apply steady force to the hard grain, thrust after thrust, turning it laboriously into flour. Their toes remain tucked under their feet for hours on end as they scoop up handfuls of stored grain onto the quern. Occasionally, they stand up and stretch, to ease their aching arms and legs. The woman we are watching closely is young, so the soreness was still tolerable. Her mother walked every day, crippled by painful arthritis, with sore arms and large toes after years of grinding and hefting baskets heavy with grain and acorns.

The people of Abu Hureyra lived in changing times. By 10,000 BCE, still-rising human populations began to match the world's capacity to support them as hunter-gatherers (Figure 6.1). For thousands of years, the problem was easy to solve—simply move elsewhere. As global temperatures warmed, people began to exploit an ever-increasing range of food resources with greater efficiency. This enabled them to avert starvation. It was also a way of protecting themselves from food shortages caused by short-term droughts and other unpredictable climatic shifts.

DOI: 10.4324/9781003177326-6

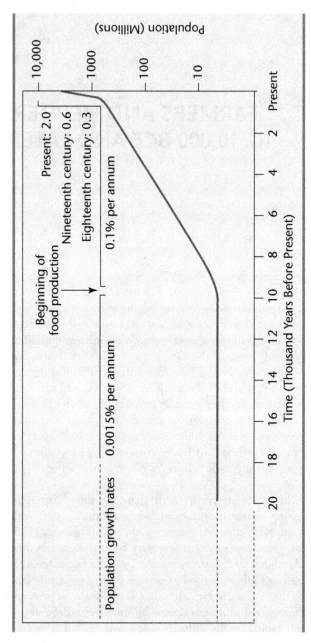

Figure 6.1 Changes in world population since the beginnings of food production. There has been an explosion in human population densities over the past 10,000 years.

More complex societies developed in a remarkable variety of environments, from fertile river valleys to coastal deserts. Increased complexity depended on several factors. Mobility constrained by geography, or the presence of neighbors being one; another, the abundant, seldom exhausted food resources, ranging from fish and mollusks, to wild seeds and nuts close at hand . Finally, population growth must have reached a point where food shortages were becoming more commonplace. This created an imbalance between people and their food supplies. By this time, the only solution was to intensify the food quest. This resulted in agriculture and animal husbandry—food production, then increased cultural complexity and a degree of social ranking.

Groups at the edges of several ecological zones could sometimes live in more-or-less permanent settlements. They turned to another strategy. They experimented with the planting of wild grasses to supplement increasingly scarce plant foods. A combination of population change and unexpected climatic shifts made it easier for their descendants to adopt new economic strategies—namely food production. This dramatic change occurred not at one location, but in numerous places around the world.

THEORIES OF THE ORIGINS OF FOOD PRODUCTION

An enormous academic literature surrounds the origins of food production, so we navigate only briefly through the major theories here. Realize at once that agriculture was not the invention of a single person. It was a major shift in adaptation to local environments where potentially domesticable animals and plants abounded.

We now have ever more detailed information on the environments in which farming began. Apart from much more accurate climatic data, we now have detailed information on ancient plant foods. Today's researchers can recover large seed samples by using flotation methods, passing occupation deposits through water and screening them. Furthermore, the study of animal bones has provided a wealth of new information on the domestication of cattle, sheep, goats, and other animals. Finally, radiocarbon dating, with its ability to date even individual seeds, has brought new precision to the study of the emergence of early farming.

What is sometimes called the 'recovery revolution' has given birth to assumptions that many factors played a role in the changeover. The most recent generation of scenarios revolve around ecology and opportunism. They talk of people turning to superior local food resources when the chance arose. All these models seek to identify the processes that caused people to shift to deliberate cultivation. This is hard, not that we lack ideas, but because field data to prove or disprove them is very hard to acquire. Ultimately, we are looking for sets of conditions that came together more-or-less simultaneously. These include population pressure, distributions of domesticable plants and animals, the rate at which environments were changing, even grass harvesting techniques. We may never be able to assemble all these sets into a case based on what actually happened in South-west Asia or elsewhere. At this stage, all we can do is describe what we know about the transition in different parts of the world.

THE CONSEQUENCES OF FOOD PRODUCTION

The new economies spread to every part of the world where food production was possible, except those of extreme aridity or where cold made agriculture or herding impossible. In some places, agriculture and stock raising were the economic base for cities and literate civilizations. But most human societies did not go further than subsistence-level food production until the machine age.

The domestication of plants and animals led to economic strategies that increased and stabilized available food supplies, although more energy was needed to produce them. Territories became smaller; people were anchored to their cultivated land and permanent settlements were commonplace. With the new economies came new social institutions involved with the inheritance and ownership of land. Previously scattered populations came together in larger settlements.

Technological developments were as important as the new economies. Housing became more durable and elaborate, the designs varying considerably with the local environment. For instance, many farmers in warmer habitats habitually slept on flat roofs during the summer. They also modified earlier toolkits for new tasks. Axes and adzes had long been used by forest peoples and now became vital for farmers. Many new axes had ground edges, which were tough and remarkably effective. At first, wooden digging sticks and stone-bladed hoes served for turning the soil, tools long used by foragers to dig up roots. Thousands of years later, iron-bladed short- or long-handled hoes came into widespread use. Eventually, the ox-drawn plow replaced hand labor, equipped first with a wooden blade, then bronze, and eventually iron. The plow was a major innovation, for it enabled farmers to turn the soil faster and to a much great depth than before. More elaborate storage became essential with only an annual harvest in most places. Grain bins, storage pits, even baskets and clay-lined silos protected grain against rodents. Clay vessels and gourds came into widespread use for carrying, cooking, and storing food.

Unlike hunting and foraging, farming transformed the environment on a large scale with tree felling, land clearance and the burning of vegetation. Voracious domestic animals cleared pastures of native grass coverage, allowing heavy rains to denude hills of valuable soil. Grazing was never the same again. The earliest farming depended heavily on careful selection of soils for cultivation, so fields were probably scattered over much wider areas than later. Farmers were also at the mercy of climatic shifts, especially low rainfall and short- and long-term drought cycles. As population densities rose, something directly linked to farming, so did the risk of hunger and longer-term famine.

Was, then, food production a real improvement in human existence? Farmers, with their sedentary settlements and high population densities were much more vulnerable to famine than their hunter-gatherer predecessors. Life expectancies may have fallen; anemia and slower growth resulting from malnutrition were commonplace. However, agriculture—resulting in increased food availability coupled with societal preferences for bigger families to provide the work force—fed the world's population growth, even if health standards and life expectancy fell.

But farming is labor intensive. Judging from numerous anthropological studies, much more work went into agriculture than hunting and gathering. Most likely, people turned to food production because they had no other alternative. There are well-documented examples of 19th- and 20th-century hunter-gatherers who were well aware of agriculture but never practiced it, among them the Australian Aborigines and California Indians. Neither of these peoples had any incentive to adopt food production, which would reduce their leisure time and produce more food than they required.

DOMESTICATING ANIMALS AND PLANTS

Hunter-gatherers always had an intimate knowledge of plants and animals, so that steps to tame them were much smaller than is often assumed. No one knows when the domestication of animals began, but it happened with highly social animals like sheep and goats, because they follow the lead of a dominant herd leader. Most early successes with animal domestication involved gregarious animals, who could be thought of as a food reserve, as "grain on the hoof." Domestication involved limiting the movement of a herd, regulating its breeding, and controlling feeding to shape future generations. As part of domestication, mutual interdependence between humans and animals increased.

Animal domestication came about in several areas of Southwest Asia at about the same time. The first species to be domesticated were goats, pigs, and sheep by about 9500 BCE. Cattle were much harder to tame, but mtDNA from cattle bones suggest they were domesticated by about 8000 BCE from a small population of females in Southwest Asia and also in Southeast Turkey. Thereafter, they spread widely into Europe and throughout the Mediterranean and African worlds.

Wild barley, wheat, and other crops were quite different from their domesticated equivalents. In the wild, such grains can be harvested simply by tapping their stems over baskets. The rachis, the hinge between the stem and the grain, is brittle in wild grasses, but sturdier in domestic grasses, requiring a sharp-edged sickle or the uprooting of an entire plant. During the early stages of domestication, people probably selected, unconsciously, grasses with a tougher rachis. Perhaps sickles or uprooting individual plants accelerated new harvesting methods. DNA fingerprints on einkorn (wheat) in Southeast Turkey have shown that grasses might have become fully domesticated within 20 to 30 years. The same DNA research has pinpointed a potential area for domestication centered on the Karacadag Mountains in Southeast Turkey.

THE EARLIEST FARMING IN SOUTHWEST ASIA (C. 10,000 TO 5000 BCE)

Ten millennia ago, major social change was under way in parts of Southwest Asia. Southeast Turkey was a highland and lowland environment that was a productive environment for hunter-gatherers by 9000 BCE – summers are hot and dry, while winters are cool and wet, with soils that support natural stands of wild cereals. This was an area where some grasses were tamed, notably einkorn, at a time when local people were engaged in increasingly sophisticated ritual observances.

GÖBEKLI TEPE AND NEVALI ÇORI (C. 9600 BCE)

Several early villages bear witness to elaborate rituals. Göbekli Tepe in southeastern Turkey was a major ceremonial center in about 9600 BCE (Figure 6.2). The inhabitants sank at least four circular structures into the limestone bedrock, giving them an almost crypt-like feel. Two huge stone pillars stood in the center of each crypt, with as many as eight others around the edges. The pillars bore carvings of animals like wild boar, wild oxen, and gazelle, also headless figures. A nearby site, Nevali Çori, yielded 29 limestone and mud houses, some of them cult buildings. Here the visitor stepped down into an interior ringed by stone benches. Once again, carved animal figures and others with human heads appear, perhaps hinting at connections between humans and the supernatural world.

Construction and ritual activities at these sites must have required dozens of people, to say nothing of large food surpluses. With their sometimes-massive standing architecture, they come as a surprise, at the cusp of agriculture. Why use so many resources? Why were they there? We can guess that some of the rituals involved honoring ancestors as well as interactions with the supernatural world. These were ritual beliefs that assumed persistent importance in the farming societies that followed.

Between 13,000 and 11,000 BCE, temperatures rose rapidly across Southwestern Asia, perhaps as much as 7°C per century. The climatic see-saw then plunged rapidly between about 11,000 and 9600 BCE. A cold snap, known to scientists as the Younger Dryas (named after a polar flower, *Dryas octopetala*), brought renewed arctic

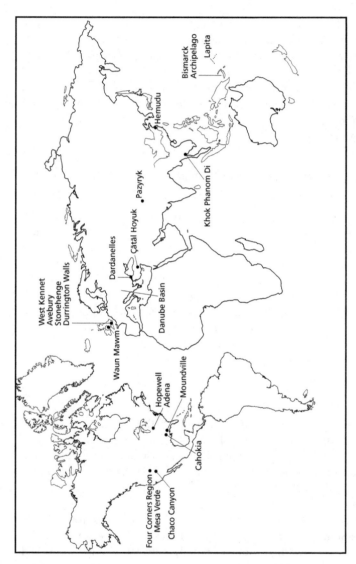

Figure 6.2 Map showing sites in Chapters 6 and 7.

vegetation to Europe and ice sheets advanced once more. The severe cold brought severe drought conditions to Southwest Asia. Winter frosts killed wild grasses and delayed the maturation of cereals. Hungry communities survived on gazelle hunting and more intensive processing of wild cereal and legumes. In areas like Southeast Turkey and northern Syria, some communities started planting wild grasses in attempts to extend their range.

ABU HUREYRA (C. 11,500 BCE) AND JERICHO (C. 10.500 BCE)

Thanks to meticulous excavation, we know a great deal about the foraging practices of the inhabitants of a small village settlement known as Abu Hureyra in Syria's Euphrates Valley. The village came into being in 11,500 BCE, a small hamlet of cramped pit dwellings with reed roofs sunk partially into the soil. For the next 1500 years, the inhabitants enjoyed a somewhat warmer and damper climate then today. They lived in a well-watered steppe habitat where wild cereal grasses abounded. There were between 300 and 400 people at Abu Hureyra as it grew, perhaps grouped into clans of people with common descent.

At Abu Hureyra, people had focused on gazelle hunting and half a dozen staple wild plants, but the village was abandoned, perhaps in part because of a firewood shortage. In about 9000 BCE, a new settlement rose on the Abu Hureyra mound. Within a generation, gazelle hunting gave way to herding sheep and goats. Wild grasses became much rarer close to the village, instead they cultivated einkorn, pulses, rye, and other cereals. The 400 or so inhabitants abandoned their community in about 8200 BCE, probably for a better watered landscape. After 7700 BCE, conditions improved; the people returned and lived in a much larger village of mudbrick houses separated by narrow alleys. Wetter conditions returned and the drier centuries were forgotten. Farming and herding spread from coast to interior, to the highlands, and into Mesopotamia and the Nile Valley.

Most early farming settlement lay on low ground near well-watered, easily cultivable land. At Jericho in the Jordan Valley, a small camp lay by a local spring by 10,500 BCE. A more permanent farming settlement quickly followed. Soon the inhabitants built massive stone walls complete with towers and a rock-cut ditch more than 2.7 meters deep. Their beehive shaped huts clustered inside the walls. Whether the city wall was to protect against people or floods is unknown. Jericho also yielded compelling evidence of an ancestor cult, in the form of human skulls with plastered faces, presumably revered ancestors. Plastered skulls and other human figurines have also come from other early farming villages.

Abu Hureyra, Jericho and other villages now dotted the South-western Asian landscape. They were part of a rapidly changing world where people became anchored to their lands and to their ancestors, the guardians of the land. We'll explore this rapidly transforming world in Chapter 7.

SUB-SAHARAN AFRICA (4000 BCE TO EARLY FIRST MILLENNIUM CE)

For thousands of years after the Ice Age, sub-Saharan Africa flourished in almost complete isolation from other societies both in the Nile Valley as well as in Northeast Africa, the Mediterranean, and the Indian Ocean world. One reason for the isolation was the Sahara Desert, which was somewhat better watered before 4000 BCE. Scattered group of herders grazed cattle and other animals on its semi-arid grasslands until increasing aridity after 4000 BCE pushed out herders to the margins of the desert, especially into the Nile Valley. Their leaders with their cattle cults are thought to have played an important part in the development of Egyptian civilization (see Chapter 10).

The southern margins of the Sahara are known as the Sahel, an Arabic term for "shore". The constantly shifting Sahel served as a shoreline between the traditional African societies south of the desert and the much more widely connected peoples to the north. Over many centuries, there were irregular contacts between north and further south, driven by a steady demand for African raw materials such as easily carved ivory and gold. These contacts with people living south of the Sahara should not surprise us. Cattle herding had a long history in the Sahel's semi-arid lands. Grazing land and reliable water supplies meant that the herders covered long distances as a matter of necessity. These contacts were but sporadic, given the aridity of the desert. It was not until much later that the camel, the so-called 'ship of the desert', made travel across the Sahara and along its southern margins more commonplace.

Food production in sub-Saharan Africa arose spontaneously, as with the indigenous domestication of the grain, teff, in the Horn of Africa; and also came to sub-Saharan Africa through numerous trade networks. Both agriculture and stock raising spread gradually into the tropics. Pearl millet, sorghum, and cowpeas spread through West Africa after 3000 BCE But the main spread of subsistence farming southward into the heart of tropical Africa originated in Central West Africa.

Beginning around 4000 to 3500 BCE. Bantu-speaking farmers replaced indigenous hunter-gatherer groups in complex, often apparently rapid, movements. They were established on the banks of the Zambezi River and in Southern Africa by 300 CE. Most details of these important population movements are still unknown, except for linguistic speculations, for there are few archaeologists working in the region. Despite this, we know that the foundations of the major African states that developed during the late first and early second millennium CE lie among Bantu-speaking peoples (see Chapter 8).

EARLY FARMERS IN ASIA (BEFORE 7000 TO 3000 BCE)

A second major center of plant domestication developed in eastern Asia, almost as early as it did in the Levant.

Rice was the staple of ancient farming over an enormous area of southern and southeastern Asia and southern China. People cultivated rice in the lowlands flanking the Yangtze River at least as early as 8000 BCE. The earliest cultivation took place in alluvial swamp areas, where there was plenty of water. Similar conditions may also have occurred on the Ganges River Plain and in the densely occupied coastal habitats of coastal southern China and Southeast Asia, where mangrove swamps abound. Here, farming communities exploited wild rice and cultivated it too, a process that lasted for many centuries. But, by 3000 BCE, much more sophisticated agricultural societies flourished along the Yangtze River and further afield. By this time, a trend toward ranked societies had taken firm hold.

In northern China, a second major center of agriculture developed along the Huang He river. Here, the staple was millet, first farmed along the lower reaches of the river between 9000 and

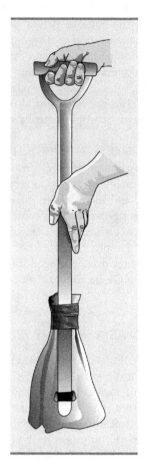

Figure 6.3 A reconstruction of a shovel-like agricultural tool, *c.* 6000 BCE. The blade was formed from a water buffalo shoulder blade.

7000 BCE. Five centuries later, the first sedentary farming villages appeared in this area. The fine, soft-textured soils of the Huang He valley could be cultivated using simple digging sticks during the summer, wet season. Many villages lay near small streams on lower river terraces, where their inhabitants cultivated several varieties of millet, sorghum, hemp, and mulberry.

The best known of China's early farming cultures is the Yangshao, which flourished over an enormous area of northern China. Each village was a self-contained community where farmers cultivated foxtail millet in riverside gardens that flooded each spring. Agriculture developed over a very wide area, with people adapting their crops and farming methods to local conditions. In time, the success of the new economies led to local population increases, more complex cultures, and the concentration of wealth in privileged hands.

EARLY AMERICAN AGRICULTURE (C. 8000 BCE ONWARD)

Food production developed independently in the Americas. Over more than ten thousand years, Native Americans had acquired a thorough knowledge of wild plants, both for food and other purposes. In some regions like the Midwest and southeastern North America, they exploited plant foods intensively. Many groups near lakes and rivers with plentiful food supplies were able to live in permanent settlements. In time, as populations rose, they also started planting wild grasses to supplement those available in the wild. Eventually, this led to agriculture, as it did in Southwest Asia and China, among other regions.

In contrast to farmers in the Old World, Native Americans domesticated few animals. In the Andes, they tamed the llama and alpacas, which provided wool. The dog, the guinea pig, the turkey, and the muscovy duck were also tamed. There were no potentially domesticated animals that could pull loads or plows.

There were three major centers of domestication in the Americas: highland and lowland Central America, for maize, beans, squash and sweet potatoes; in the central Andes highlands, people grew root crops like potatoes and manioc; Southeastern North Americans cultivated pepo squash, sunflowers, and other local plants.

BEANS, MAIZE AND SQUASH IN CENTRAL AMERICA (C. 8000 BCE AND LATER)

The process of domestication is still little understood. Most likely, the changeover came about as people developed strategies to cope with continuous short-term climatic shifts and growing populations. At Guilá Naquitz rock shelter in Mexico's Valley of Oaxaca, occupied about six times between 8750 and 6670 BCE, the inhabitants experimented with wild beans in wet years, but they eventually relied ever more heavily on their bean crops. They were growing squashes as early as 8000 BCE and eventually also cultivated a simple form of maize. This kind of changeover occurred in many parts of Central America.

Today, over 150 varieties of maize (*Zea mays*) are grown both as food and cattle fodder—the most important food crop in the Americas. The wild ancestor is teosinte, a grass that still grows in Central America. Domestication may have occurred unintentionally, as foragers favored the most harvestable, and most maize-like, of teosinte grasses, and those whose seeds scattered less easily when ripe. In time, they began to weed such teosinte stands, then deliberately planted the more useful varieties. Eventually the grass became dependent on human intervention and genetic changes led to maize.

The earliest known maize comes from the Rio Balsas region of southwestern Mexico, where it was grown as early as 6700 BCE and was well established 1700 years later. In the San Marcos Cave in southern Mexico's Tehuacán Valley, maize was grown by at least 3600 BCE. The earliest cobs preserved in dry caves are less than 20 millimeters long and could not disperse their kernels naturally—a clear sign of full domestication.

The eight-rowed maize, *Maiz de Ocho,* found at Tehuacán, was the common ancestral corn that spread thousands of kilometers from its original homeland. Subsequent derivatives of this basic maize developed throughout the Americas. If archaeologist Kent Flannery and other specialists are correct, plant domestication in Central America was not so much an invention as a shift in ecological adaptation. This was a deliberate choice by peoples living in areas where economic strategies necessitated intensive exploitation of plant foods.

Although this chapter focuses on staple grains, two Mesoamerican fruits deserve a footnote: the tomato, and the calorie-rich avocado. The precise domestication timelines of both remain unclear, but we know that by 500 BCE the tomato was being cultivated in southern Mexico, and surrounding areas. Tomatoes, the edible berries of the plant *Solanum lycopersicum*, were originally the size of peas. It was the Aztecs of central Mexico, among others, who developed the larger, sweeter, bright red version that we know today. A much-revered fruit, the Pueblo peoples of Mesoamerica (*c.* 1000 CE) gave the tomato almost mystical powers, believing those who ingested its seeds were blessed with powers of divination. Avocados may also have originated in Mexico, specifically the fertile Tehuacán Valley. There they were being eaten by locals from around 10,000 to 9000 years ago, as suggested by the discovery of the oldest-known avocado pit—found in the region's Coxcatlan Cave. Several other caves in the valley have similar avocado pits, though not quite as early. The undomesticated version was small, with dark black skin and large pits. Its subsequent domestication may have begun as early as 5000 BCE.

SOUTH AMERICA: HIGHLANDS AND COAST (C. 8000 BCE AND LATER)

The same shift toward domesticated plant food and intensive agriculture occurred in the mountain highlands of the Andes and along the low-lying, arid Pacific coast. A great variety of animals and wild plants abounded in the harsh and varied landscape of Andes peaks and mountain valleys. The farmers only domesticated a fraction of these potential crops, some of which had been domesticated in the highlands by almost 8000 BCE. Apart from llamas, domesticated along the coast and in the highlands, maybe as early as 2500 BCE, alpacas, also guinea pigs, were cherished for their wool and as food. Three highland crops became staples—potatoes, quinoa, and ulluco, between 3000 and 2000 BCE, perhaps earlier.

The Peruvian coast forms a narrow strip at the foot of the Andes and is one of the driest places on earth. For thousands of years, coastal groups had exploited the inshore anchovy fisheries, so rich that they fostered permanent settlement. Fishing may have assumed great importance after 5000 BCE, when the climate was warmer and drier than today. The rivers that flowed down from the mountains onto deep, rich soils, and brought plentiful water for part of the year. By 5000 BCE, people were cultivating cotton, squash, peppers and tuberous begonias in the coastal valleys.

Fish and mollusks were staples, then maize spread into South America by at least 3000 BCE. Within a short time, more complex farming societies developed out of the simple coastal village communities of earlier times. Effective adaptations to challenging local environments developed in some areas of the coast. Farming and fishing societies became elaborate chiefdoms, then wealthy, volatile states based on fertile river valleys and irrigation agriculture (see Chapters 8 and 13).

This is a chapter about profound cultural change, which resulted from what was arguably the most significant development in human history—the moment at which, for the first time, people in various parts of the world changed from hunting and foraging to growing and herding their own food. The consequences for humanity were momentous.

★★★

Paloma, coastal Peru, 2000 BCE... The reed canoes hover close off-shore on the calm, cloudy day. A sluggish swell barely moves them, but their paddlers are busy with reed baskets. Thousands of small fish, anchovies, crowd one another in a belt, their noses projecting above the surface. The belt of fish extends for about a kilometer, making the ocean look like chain mail, chased inshore by larger and voracious enemies close offshore. Heavily laden canoes piled with baskets skillfully come ashore; within moments, the crew exchange full baskets for empty ones and paddle back to the shoal of ancho-vies. On the beach, women and children process the catch, laying it out to dry. At the nearby settlement, some weave fine cotton nets, which last a long time in salt water. A few kilometers inshore, other villagers, who are not fishers, grow cotton and exchange it for anchovy and sardine meal in baskets and bags.

FURTHER READING

General works: Graeme Barker, *The Agricultural Revolution in Prehis-tory* (Oxford: Oxford University Press, 2006); Peter Bellwood, *The First Farmers: The Origins of Agricultural Societies* (New York: Wiley Blackwell, 2004); Bruce D. Smith, *The Emergence of Agriculture*, 2nd ed. (New York: W.H. Freeman, 1998). Andrew Moore, *Village on the Euphrates* (New York: Oxford University Press, 2000) is a meticulous account of Abu Hureyra. Ian Hodder, *The Leopard's Tale* (London: Thames & Hudson, 2006) is a fascinating analysis of the beliefs behind Çatalhöyük. Europe: I.J. Thorpe, *The Origins of Agri-culture in Europe* (Abingdon: Routledge, 1996). Early Chinese food production: Li Liu, *The Chinese Neolithic* (Cambridge: Cambridge University Press, 2004). Maize: Michael Blake, *Maize for the Gods: Unearthing the 9,000-Year History of Corn* (Berkeley: University of California Press, 2015).

VILLAGES, TOWNS, AND CHIEFS (AFTER ABOUT 8000 BCE)

The Dardanelles, eastern Mediterranean, 5500 BCE... Generations of farmers have cultivated and fished along the shores of the narrow saltwater bay. Many of their villages cluster on the far side of a low ridge that overlooks a large freshwater lake, which extends to the horizon. But the landscape is changing. The salt water bay becomes larger every year as the sea level rises and water creeps over closer to the top of the ridge. Nearby villagers still fish in salt water and fresh, but the talk over their fires revolves around what will happen next. Then a major winter storm brings steep waves and howling winds. The Dardanelles surges over the ridge, first merely a minor channel. But the down gradient accelerates the storm waters. The narrow defile becomes a torrent that carries land and houses, people and farmland with it. The survivors flee for their lives to higher ground and take shelter with kin. Within months, the freshwater lake has become a brackish sea—now the Black Sea.

ÇATALHÖYÜK (7400 TO 5700 BCE)

Çatalhöyük in Central Turkey was a village, if not almost a town, for nearly 2000 years, between 7,400 and 5700 BCE (see Figure 6.2). Generations of families occupied tightly packed, flat-roofed houses entered from above, separated by narrow alleys. Here, respect for the

DOI: 10.4324/9781003177326-7

ancestors weighed heavily on the inhabitants. It came into being as a closely packed village when such settlements had flourished for more than a millennium. Its long life and prosperity stemmed in part from its strategic location close to major sources of toolmaking obsidian near Lake Van in eastern Turkey. The tentacles of the obsidian trade extended hundreds of kilometers along the eastern Mediterranean coast and as far as the Persian Gulf.

At its greatest extent, the village covered 37.4 hectares atop a large mound. Numerous small houses built of sun-dried brick backed onto one another. Their roofs were flat, the walls forming a convenient fortification for the settlement. The village was rebuilt at least 18 times over 1400 years. The inhabitants never built large public buildings or shrines, or specialized production areas. Everything revolved round the houses and occasional small courtyards.

Çatalhöyük was a social jigsaw, without temples, but with a few special dwellings, where the revered ancestors weighed heavily on visitors. The excavators call them "History Houses", prompted by the paintings on their walls that display elaborate symbolism, including paintings of humans and dangerous animals, sometimes animal/ humans. Numerous burials lay beneath them, in one case 62 bodies spanning a 40-year occupation, compared with an average of 5 to 8 bodies. Each of these structures had historical significance. The inhabitants even dug under the floors to recover the long buried skulls of bulls, a beast of profound symbolic importance. There was also a strong tradition of passing skulls of ancestors down from one generation to the next. Plastered skulls of humans and bulls were displayed on important occasions such as the founding of a house (Figure 7.1).

The people who lived in these houses lived much the same way as everyone else. They were guardians of history, religion, and ancestors. The same individuals may also have played an important role in ceremonial feasts involving wild bulls that had mythical and spiritual associations. Ancestors, human and animal, protected the dead, the house, and its inhabitants. Associations between dangerous animals, headless humans, and birds—all these motifs were part of a strong tradition of continuity that was a central part of societies like that based at Çatalhöyük. There were broadly similar beliefs and traditions over a large area of Southwestern Asia at the time.

Figure 7.1 Hypothetical reconstruction of the east and south walls of a shrine in a "History House" at Çatalhöyük, with sculpted ox heads, horns, benches, and relief models of bulls and rams. One entered by ladder from the roof.

Not that Çatalhöyük was necessarily a pleasant place to live. What began as a small village in 7400 BCE became a densely populated community that could almost be called a town. Inevitably, chronic overcrowding and poor hygiene led to infections, which appear on the bones of the dead. Crowding also led to violence, reflected in the remains of people wounded or killed, often with hard clay balls; many of the victims were women.

Çatalhöyük was a bustling community, sufficiently versatile that the people could switch from cattle to sheep and goats during a prolonged cold, dry cycle between 6325 and 5815 BCE. By 5700 BCE, when it was finally abandoned, farming had begun on the Aegean Islands and in Greece and parts of southeastern Europe.

Many larger settlements in Southwest Asia became trading centers. The quantity of imported materials and exotic objects found in communities large and small increased dramatically after 8000 BCE. Farmers not only used obsidian from Anatolia, they exchanged turquoise from Syria, and seashells from the Mediterranean and the Red Sea. As economic activity picked up and agricultural methods improved, in part because of technological innovation, so the stage was set for the emergence of the first urban civilizations (see Chapter 8).

EUROPE: ANCESTORS AND SACRED LANDSCAPES

Farming spread into southeastern Europe some 2,000 years after it appeared in Southwest Asia. Until recently, most people assumed that it was a simple process of colonization that effectively terminated hunter-gatherer societies throughout Europe. In fact, the process was far more complicated, and included a mixture of both innovations brought by immigrants and local adaptations to changing conditions and new neighbors.

Farmers were present in what is now Greece as early as 7000 BCE. They cultivated easily farmed floodplain lands, planting emmer wheat and barley, and herding cattle, sheep, and pigs. By 5500 BCE, farming communities were commonplace in Greece and along the Dalmatian coast of the Adriatic Sea. Within a few centuries, sheep herding and sedentary agriculture were well established along the Mediterranean coast and inland.

To the north, Europe's temperate zones had year-round rainfall and marked seasonal contrasts between summer and winter. Here, farmers built their houses of timber, with thatched roofs. Fortunately for them, their arrival coincided with a warm, moist phase, when midsummer temperatures were at least 2°C warmer than today. The actual number of newcomers may have been very small, with indigenous hunter-gatherers adapting readily to the new economies.

In about 5500 BCE, the rising Mediterranean flooded the glacial Euxine Lake, now the Black Sea. The inundation must have disrupted coastal farming communities over a wide area. This was when cattle herding and spring-sown cereal farming developed across large areas of continental Europe, especially on soils formed from soft, wind-blown glacial deposits known as loess. Hunter-gatherer societies continued to flourish in areas that were marginal for farming or herding.

The spread of farming across Europe was a stop-start process that involved major cultural changes over many centuries. The best known early European farming culture is the Bandkeramik (or Danubian), which emerged in the Danube Basin around 5300 BCE.

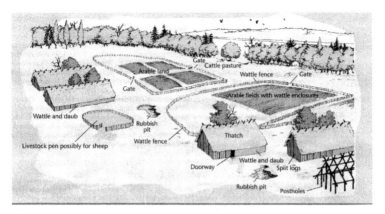

Figure 7.2 Reconstruction of a Bandkeramik farming complex in Central Europe showing long houses and field boundaries.

Cattle and smaller stock, like sheep and goats, were an important part of Bandkeramik life. So were cereal crops like barley, einkorn and emmer wheat. These the farmers cultivated using crop rotation and fallowing. This enabled them to occupy villages of 50 to 60 people for long periods of time (Figure 7.2). Bandkeramik communities thrived as far west as the southern Netherlands by 4800 BCE. Eventually local farming adaptations replaced hunting and gathering in southern Scandinavia and lowland Britain.

Eventually, Bandkeramik communities dwelt in clusters of large, permanent, timber long houses occupied over long periods of time. Cherished kin ties linked villages over wide areas. Many Bandkeramik graves contain richly adorned female bodies. This may mean that women had high status and considerable political power.

COMMUNAL BURIAL AND MEGALITHS

During the fifth millennium BCE, more elaborate burial customs emerged throughout Europe, especially in the west, where communal tombs came into fashion. These included the so-called "megaliths," communal burial places fashioned from rough-hewn boulders and buried under earthen mounds. Such corporate burial places may have been where revered kin leaders were buried, also people with close genealogical ties to the ancestors. Some farmers in today's France were building large communal megalithic tombs as early as 4500 BCE. Such structures came into widespread use throughout western Europe and western Mediterranean lands. Quite what they signified has been much debated, without any firm conclusions. In southern Britain, people were buried under long barrows, many of which had boulder interiors. The West Kennet long barrow near Avebury in southern England was used as a communal grave over several generations around 3500 BCE. Perhaps such monuments served as territorial markers in an increasingly crowded farming landscape, where they commemorated ancestral ownership of the surrounding land. As time went on, burial ceremonies and commemoration of the ancestors may have revolved around even larger monuments, the so-called henges, stone- and wood-built circles, described below.

Between 2800 and 2400 BCE, both individual graves and communal sepulchers came into use in Central and eastern Europe. This was the moment when new beliefs reinforced individual power and prestige. Now a powerful individual buried with elaborate grave furniture became the sole male ancestor, the foundation of authority over land ownership. This became hereditary and inheritance of land and wealth was legitimized.

The changeover coincided roughly with the widespread introduction of the plow into European agriculture in about 2600 BCE. This development coincided with the use of oxen for traction, also sheep shearing and horse riding, with major changes in land ownership. Much more land was now cleared. Both household production and kin ties gave way to societies where individual success, prestige, and inheritance of land were the norm.

AVEBURY AND STONEHENGE (C. 2550 TO 1500 BCE)

Great monuments like Stonehenge and nearby Avebury did not stand alone. Avebury stands at the center of a vast, long-vanished landscape marked by burial mounds, enclosures, charnel houses for the dead, and other sites that commemorate the ancestors. Avebury was built in about 2550 BCE, comprising a stone circle with enclosure and ditch covering 11.5 hectares. Ninety-eight standing stones stood within the outer circle. When newly constructed in the white chalk subsoil, Avebury would have been visible for many kilometers, the center of a huge sacred landscape with earthworks and burial mounds, like West Kennet, on a nearby ridge.

The annual round of ritual observances at places like Avebury and Stonehenge reinforced the continuity of human life. This was when the megaliths became important symbols of political and social continuity during a period of significant population growth.

Stonehenge, one of the most famous archaeological sites in the world, began as a circle of ritual pits in about 2950 BCE. After frequent reconstructions, the celebrated stone circles appeared soon after 2500 BCE, made from bluestones, large and small, imported from South Wales some 240 kilometers away and sarsen stone from about 30 kilometers away. However, these bluestones were not just any old rocks. Latest research has revealed that the builders of Stonehenge took (or "reappropriated") stones from an existing stone circle at Waun Mawm in the Preseli Hills of South Wales (today represented by only four stones). On excavating the erstwhile circle's now-empty stone-holes, archaeologist Mike Parker Pearson found they matched those of the Stonehenge bluestones—one hole even bore the impress of a stone of unusual form known at Stonehenge, fitting "like a key in a lock". Were the builders transferring mystical powers from the Preseli Hills to Stonehenge? Whatever the case, this seems to have been a process of immense ritual significance.

At Stonehenge, generations of builders tinkered with the circles and their distinctive trilithons. The significance of the circles eludes us, but they are oriented toward the summer and winter solstices, important points in the agricultural cycle that governed local life. Stonehenge was an important place, redolent with symbolism, but it was part of a much larger ancient landscape of a long avenue, burial mounds, and other features. A large earthen circle and ditch complex known as Durrington Walls lies 3.2 kilometers northeast of Stonehenge. Inside the circle stood two large cult houses, where the ritual leaders dwelt. Numerous houses lay outside the circle, part of what was once a very large village.

Mike Parker Pearson believes that the Stonehenge landscape encompassed two symbolic realms. One was Stonehenge with its stone circles, a permanent monument to the dead and the ancestors. Whereas by contrast, Durrington Walls was a realm of the living, a place of transitory existence. There are many animal bones at Durrington, as if feasting was commonplace. Stonehenge is more austere, the two linked by ceremonial avenues that served as processional ways at the solstices.

By about 2500 BCE, bronze metallurgy was in widespread use across Europe, the alloying of copper and tin having been developed independently of Southwest Asia in Southeast Europe. Between 1700 and 1300 BCE, rapid technological innovation occurred, much of it because of dramatically expanded trade, not only in metal ores, but also in prestigious objects of many kinds. Society was changing, too, as local monopolies over salt and other critical materials developed. Almost inevitably, wealth became more focused in the hands of a comparatively few individuals. Ambitious, powerful chieftains carved out ever-changing alliances through centuries of considerable political instability.

Militant elites appeared, like one group of warriors in western Hungary, known to archaeologists as the Urnfield people, because of their fortified villages and large cemeteries filled with cremated burials. Urnfield people made full use of horse-drawn vehicles and much more elaborate weaponry such as swords and body armor using sheet metal. Urnfield weaponry and burial rites spread far west through temperate Europe. New, more consolidated agriculture allowed the cultivation of much heavier soils for the first time. Cattle and other animals were fully integrated into the food producing economy, while sheep were bred as much for their wool as their flesh.

By the first millennium BCE, the vast rolling grassland and steppe that extended from the Ukraine as far east as China had long been home to groups of horse-using nomads and their herds. Three thousand years ago, the first Scythian nomads appear in history, formidable warriors who lived in felt tents. In northeastern Siberia, chiefs with elaborate tattoos, dressed in leather and woolen garments, lay under burial mounds. At Pazyryk in the Altai mountains of Siberia, near to the frontier between China and Russia, peculiar climatic conditions preserved—deep-frozen in solid ice—the contents of a Scythian chief's tomb. Dated to the 5th century BCE, the chief was accompanied to the next world by his wife, servants, horses, food, and chariots. Exuberant stylized animal art adorned the chief's tattooed skin, his weapons and harnesses.

The steppe people lived to the north of well-traveled trade routes and the settled lands of western Asian farmers. Enormous territories could only support small numbers of nomads. The frontiers of settled lands ebbed and flowed with the generations, as nomads encroached on farming land, searching for grazing for their herds.

RICE FARMERS IN ASIA AND PACIFIC VOYAGING (AFTER 5000 BCE)

Numerous farming cultures flourished in southern China. The Hemudu people, who lived south of modern Shanghai, dwelt in part in a marshy habitat surrounded by forests and ponds. Between 5000 and 4500 BCE, the Hemudu site itself supported a vigorous community of rice farmers, who lived in well-built timber buildings and used bone shovels and hoes in their fields. By 4900 BCE, rice was growing in importance as a staple, relative to such plant foods as acorns or water chestnuts. From southern China, it seems that rice agriculture spread from there into India and Southeast Asia.

Quite when rice agriculture took hold in Southeast Asia is unknown, but we know it was well established in Vietnam's Red River Valley by 2500 BCE. Between 2000 and 1400 BCE, a major settlement came into being close to coastal mangrove swamps at Khok Phanom Di in Thailand. This was a wealthy community, which yielded the burial of a woman in her mid-thirties, who was an expert potter.

Offshore from mainland Asia, one enters a very different world, where root crops like taro became staples in the Bismarck Archipelago region by 1900 to 1500 BCE. The question of how the offshore Pacific islands were first settled has fascinated scientists since Captain Cook's voyages in the 18th century. Settlement of the offshore islands depended on the cultivation of root crops like taro and yams, also breadfruit, coconuts, and sugarcane. Chickens, dogs, and pigs were domesticated in mainland Asia, but were essential for survival on islands where wild foods were in short supply. As we have seen, the Solomon Islands and other islands close to New Guinea were settled during the late Ice Age. But colonization further offshore depended not only on deep water canoes, but on foods and small animals that could be transported for days in such watercraft; these voyages depended on expert pilotage and navigation.

The colonization of Melanesia took about six centuries between 1550 to 1000 BCE, achieved in seaworthy outrigger canoes. The occupation was in the hands of the Lapita people (named after an archaeological site on New Caledonia). Lapita skippers were expert traders, whose origins may have lain on the southeast Asian mainland, but whose homeland was the Bismarck Archipelago off New Guinea. They carried obsidian from New Britain Island 3700 kilometers eastward to Fiji and westward to Borneo. Their exchange networks extended over more than 8,100 kilometers, deep into the Central Pacific.

Trading networks and connections changed constantly as Lapita canoes traded as far eastward as Fiji and Tonga. These were expert navigators with an intimate knowledge of winds, weather, and ocean swells, who used the sun and stars to cross open water out of sight of land. Pilotage expertise passed down the generations by chants and oral tradition.

The settlement of Micronesia and Polynesia came much later, with a dramatic burst of ocean voyaging between 1000 and 1300 CE. Canoes arrived at uninhabited Tahiti by 1025 CE and at remote Rapa Nui by 1263 CE. A mere three centuries of ocean voyaging took people to Hawai'i by 1219 and 1269 CE. Far to the south, Polynesians arrived on remote New Zealand between 1230 and 1280 CE.

These great ocean voyages were the last chapter in the 100,000-year journey of *Homo sapiens* across the world.

ANCESTRAL PUEBLO IN THE AMERICAN SOUTHWEST (C. 2000 BCE AND LATER)

Few ancient societies were so well preadapted to agriculture as the peoples of the American Southwest and eastern woodlands. In the semi-arid southwest, with its irregular rainfall, hunting and foraging were always high-risk ventures. Domesticated plants like maize and beans had low yields in these dry environments, but they had one advantage: they were predictable food sources.

Maize first entered the Southwest during a period of higher rainfall between 2000 and 1500 BCE. Many groups first grew corn and beans as supplements to wild foods, as it helped them maximize the potential of their environments. Cultivation was never easy, for maize was close to the limits of its range here. Farmers selected moisture-retaining soils very carefully, using north- and east-facing slopes that received little direct sun. They planted near canyon mouths and diverted water from streams and springs, while dispersing their gardens to minimize risks of local droughts or floods. As local maize strains became more productive, they became a vital staple. Many groups now lived in permanent hamlets and much smaller territories. These became part of more complex societies that adapted to ever-changing climatic conditions with remarkable flexibility.

By 300 BCE, Southwestern societies depended much more heavily on agriculture. At first, many Ancestral Pueblo groups lived in small villages of pithouses. But after 900 CE much of the population congregated in above-ground settlements of adjoining rooms. These became the famous pueblos, often clustered in small arcs to make them equidistant from subterranean ceremonial rooms—*kivas.* The largest, most spectacular pueblos developed in densely population locations, such as Chaco Canyon in New Mexico, and in the Four Corners region of the northern Southwest.

CHACO CANYON, NEW MEXICO (C. 800 TO 1130 CE)

The San Juan Basin covers much of northwestern New Mexico and adjacent parts of Colorado, Utah, and Arizona. This is a landscape of broad plains and valleys, with subdued relief. Small mesas, buttes, and short canyons define the Basin. Between about 800 and 1130 CE, Chaco Canyon with its dramatic cliffs was a magnet for human settlement and ritual activity. A series of large pueblos, known commonly as "great houses", rose along the seventeen-kilometer length of the stream that flows through the canyon. Each great house was a vibrant place, where factionalism and social tensions were routine.

Pueblo Bonito is the best known. A semi-circle of rooms press on a central plaza with its once-below-ground circular ceremonial rooms, or kivas. The site itself came into being at what may have been a sacred spot, marked by striking rock formations in the nearby canyon walls (Figure 7.3).

Initially, between 860 and 935, Pueblo Bonito was a small stone-built settlement, a modest, arc-shaped place, but apparently with strong spiritual associations. The inhabitants dwelt in a layered world—the sky, the earth, and the underworld. Their village was the *sipapu,* the point of emergence from the underworld. Elaborate rituals revolved around the summer and winter solstices; the passages of the sun and

Figure 7.3 Pueblo Bonito, Chaco Canyon, New Mexico. The circular structures are subterranean *kivas*.

Alamy Stock Photo

moon. The Pueblo world was always one of harmony and order, whose basic values were reenacted in dramatic performances. The group mattered more than the individual; people focused on maintaining a human existence that had always been the same and would be similar in the future. Chaco life revolved around maize agriculture and religious belief in a landscape where the harsh realities of an arid environment defined human existence. Bonito had started as a residential settlement, but then became a great house, a ceremonial building with powerful ritual and political associations, plenty of storage space, but few permanent inhabitants, though crowded with visitors at the solstices and other major events.

Powerful ritual associations tied to the elite occupants of Chaco's great houses underscored both farming and water management. Descent through the female line, confirmed by DNA studies of burials at Pueblo Bonito, was a vital factor in the success of Chaco agriculture. Women had powerful voices in water management, their ritual activities tied to both fertility and to water. Complex systems of artificial channels and earthen canals formed part of a multifaceted irrigation system tailored to local conditions. Rapidly changing rainfall patterns and the unpredictable environment required nimble social responses to fluctuating water supplies.

Pueblo Bonito's leadership was hereditary, religious, and powerful. The cultural order reflected unpredictable environmental conditions and climate change. But it was lightly incised into the landscape. Social controls that ensured the monitoring of soils and changing water supplies, and the deployment of labor at short notice, were essential elements in the risk management that lay behind long-term survival.

In the final analysis, what made Chaco society succeed was not so much its powerful leaders but the complex obligations of kin, reciprocity, and labor for the common good. No one could be self-sufficient in an arid environment like the San Juan Basin, which is one major reason why elaborate ceremonial observances held society together.

A major drought cycle between 1130 and 1180 led to Chaco's decline, as people moved northward and elsewhere. The mid-1200s saw Mesa Verde and other pueblos in the Four Corners region achieve prominence. But drought in the 13th century saw people move away gradually, many to wetter regions in the southeast.

ADENA, HOPEWELL, AND MISSISSIPPIAN (C. 2000 BCE TO 1650 CE)

Like those in the Southwest, hunter-gatherers in North America's eastern woodlands had acquired exceptional expertise with plant foods thousands of years before sporadic cultivation of native plants like goosefoot and marsh elder began around 2000 BCE. At about the same time, the first signs of social ranking appeared in local burials. This was also when an increasing preoccupation with burial and life after death came into play.

As the centuries passed, the funeral rites associated with death and the passage from the living world to the realm of the ancestors became ever more elaborate and important. This elaboration coincided with increasing social complexity. An explosion in long-distance exchange ensued, along with the building of ceremonial earthworks.

Many centuries of long-distance exchange between neighboring communities conferred high value on certain raw materials and exotic objects in societies that valued prestige. Hammered copper objects and conch shells from the Gulf of Mexico and the Atlantic coast became symbols of high status and were buried with their owners. By 500 BCE, such individuals were interred under large burial mounds. Between 500 BCE and about 400 CE, the Adena culture flourished in the Ohio Valley, marked by elaborate ceremonial enclosures and burial mounds where important people lay in log-lined tombs.

A development of the Adena named the Hopewell tradition followed around 200 BCE and flourished for six centuries. This was an elaboration of Adena religious ideology with burial strategies that spread as far as Louisiana, northern Wisconsin, and New York State. Long-distance trade carried copper from the Great Lakes region, obsidian from as far away as Yellowstone, and shiny mica from southern Appalachia. Hopewell communities dwelt in relatively small settlements and used the simplest of technologies. All the wealth and creative skill of society was lavished on a relatively few individuals—and their lives after death.

This was a society where ceremonial objects of all kinds passed from hand to hand over long distances. Carved soapstone pipe bowls, thin mica head and breast ornaments decorated with animal and human motifs, copper axe and beads; these prized manufactures passed from one person to another through vast networks of gift-giving transactions that linked different kin leaders in lasting, important obligations to one another. Unsurprisingly, Hopewell mounds and burial complexes were far more elaborate. Some burial mounds were 12 meters high, often atop earthen platforms where people were buried over several generations. All this ceremonial reflects a complex relationship with the forces of the spiritual world and the ancestors.

The center of religious and political power shifted southward after 400 CE as the Hopewell tradition declined. This was when the people of the increasingly densely populated Mississippi floodplain gradually turned to maize as a high-yielding food staple, especially when combined with beans during the late first millennium. The new crops added to food surpluses acquired from growing native plants, fishing, and waterfowl. Major economic and social change came with the appearance of the Mississippian tradition, its greatest elaboration in the American Bottom across the river from today's St. Louis.

By 1000 CE, a large ceremonial center developed at Cahokia. At 30.5 meters high, Monk's Mound dominates a complex of mounds and plazas, once surrounded by a stockade. A powerful elite ruled over Cahokia and its hinterland. The entire ceremonial complex, which symbolized the cosmology of the region, covered more than 80 hectares, with densely populated communities surrounding it. The great center lay at a strategic point close to the Mississippi and near its confluence with the Missouri, in a region where northern and southern trade routes met. The ruling families of Cahokia achieved enormous political and spiritual power within a few generations, perhaps because of their perceived influence in the spiritual world. But they must also have been adept traders with significant economic and political connections over a wide area.

Cahokia was the most elaborate of all Mississippian chiefdoms, a major gathering point for major seasonal rituals. But its core territory was miniscule compared with that of, say, the Ancient Egyptians. Politically volatile and based on ancient religious beliefs, its power and prosperity depended on the authority, charisma, and ability of a handful of chiefs. There may well have been serious political and social tensions between the local people and the many immigrants who flocked to Cahokia, identified from isotopic analysis of teeth in burials. The great center disintegrated in about 1300 CE, for complex, and much debated, reasons. These may have included drought and social disorder. Another major center developed to the south at Moundville, in modern Alabama. The chiefs who presided over Moundville and numerous smaller centers were probably hereditary leaders. They controlled long-distance trade, and were intermediaries between the living, and ancestors, and the supernatural realm.

The great Mississippian centers were past the height of their powers when European explorers reached the Mississippi during the 16th century. If undisturbed by outsiders, would the Mississippian and its successors have developed into a fully-fledged state like the Maya and the Aztec to the south? Most experts believe they would not, because of the brief growing season and harsh climate.

Throughout the world, the most important consequences of food production were a long-term trend toward greater political elaboration, a degree of social ranking, and great interdependency in a wide range of village farming societies. In some places, such societies morphed into the pre-industrial civilizations of the past, described in the chapters that follow.

★★★

Approaching Rapi Nui, Polynesia, 1263 CE... The large outrigger canoe sails quietly through the ocean swell as the sun rises and the stars fade. For hours, the pilot has stood astride, moving effortlessly with the pitching hulls. He is silent, eyes closed, feeling the water moving beneath him. His attention quickens and he gestures to the helmsman to steer slightly to the left. He has detected a gentle cross swell from invisible cliffs at an angle to the bow. The crew awakens as a small island appears far ahead. No one is surprised, for they've trusted the pilot's judgment for days. As the canoe approaches land and alters course for a sandy beach, the men grab their spears, watchful for hostile islanders. But their landing is unopposed, the island apparently uninhabited. This is hardly surprising, for this is one of the remotest land masses on earth.

FURTHER READING

Stonehenge for the Ancestors: Part 1: Landscape and Monuments (The Stonehenge Riverside Project) by Mike Parker Pearson et al., 2020 (London: Sidestone Press, 2013) has all the latest; or for a more general book, see *Stonehenge—A New Understanding: Solving the Mysteries of the Greatest Stone Age Monument,* again by Mike Parker Pearson (London: The Experiment, 2014). On the role of religion and ritual in the emergence of complex societies, see *Religion in the Emergence of Civilization: Çatalhöyük as a Case Study,* a multi-disciplinary work edited by Ian Hodder (Cambridge: Cambridge University Press, 2011). For Chaco Canyon, turn to Brian Fagan's *Chaco Canyon: Archaeologists Explore the Lives of an Ancient Society* (New York: Oxford University Press, 2005). Cahokia: Timothy R. Pauketat, *Cahokia: Ancient America's Great City on the Mississippi* (New York: Penguin, 2009).

SUMERIANS AND ASSYRIANS (C. 3100 TO 612 BCE)

Uruk, southern Mesopotamia, 2400 BCE... The narrow street jostles with people and beasts. Heavily laden donkeys push through the crowds, their drivers close behind. A cacophony of voices echoes off the mud-brick house walls pressing on the narrow defile. Merchants in a neighboring alley tout shipments of textiles and charcoal. Guards with clubs protect a high official on a donkey making his way to the great ziggurat, parting the thong with sticks and loud cries. Women pass quietly homeward from the market with bundles of grain and dried fish. A jumble of smells assault the senses—rotting river catches, sewage, the acrid scent of animal urine, smoke from innumerable hearths, fresh cow dung. Uruk is never quiet, its people vibrant, but quarrelsome, quick to take offense, and constantly alert for a profit.

Three quarters of a century ago, Vere Gordon Childe wrote of two defining revolutions in human prehistory. We've already discussed the Agricultural Revolution. The second was the Urban Revolution, which he dated to about 3000 BCE, centered in Mesopotamia and Egypt, marked by the appearance of the first cities and writing—civilization.

CIVILIZATIONS AND CITIES

Today, we use the term *civilization* as shorthand for urbanized, state-level societies. Those described in these pages are sometimes called

DOI: 10.4324/9781003177326-8

"preindustrial civilizations" because they relied on manual labor rather than fossil fuels such as coal.

There were numerous differences between the world's pre-industrial civilizations. But they tended to share a number of common features:

- They were based on cities, either compact, or with more dispersed, populations. They had complex social organizations and were based on larger territories rather than kin-based villages or small towns.
- Their economies depended on centralized accumulation of capital and social status through tribute and taxation. This type of economy allowed the state to support hundreds, often thousands, of non-food producers such as artisans or priests. Long-distance trade, division of labor, and craft specialization were characteristic of early states.
- Metallurgy, more sophisticated agricultural methods, often including irrigation systems, came into use.
- Formal record-keeping, usually some form of written script, simple mathematics and science.
- Impressive public buildings and monumental architecture, like Egyptian temples and Maya ceremonial centers.
- Some form of state religion, in which the ruler played a leading role. For instance, the Egyptian pharaoh was considered a living god.

We should never think of the development of pre-industrial civilizations as yet one more step on a simple evolutionary ladder. Cities and states came into being as a result of complex, still little understood processes. Among these were the unintended results of ever more intensive relationships and contacts between people that connected them with one another at times of rapid population growth. The result was often a completely new form of human settlement— the city.

Today's city is a symbol of the modern industrial world, sometimes with a population in the millions. Some of the earliest urban complexes were little more than agglomerations of villages, each with their own kin loyalties. A working definition talks about cities as settlements with more than 5,000 people, but this is inadequate.

Cities have economic and organizational complexities that are distinctive. Here's a quick summary:

- A large and relatively dense population: Small cities in the ancient world had as few as 2,000 to 3,000 inhabitants. The largest such as Rome, or Changan in China, may have had more than a million.
- Specialization and interdependence, both within the city and its surrounding hinterland: The city was a central place, which depended on surrounding communities for food, but provided services for them, usually including a market for selling produce.
- Organizational complexity well beyond that of a small farming community: This linked them to a state, which also had centralized organization.
- The power of kin groups was reduced.

THE ORIGINS OF STATES

Today, we have much more data than V. Gordon Childe, which means that theorizing about the origin of states has intensified. Everyone agrees that large food surpluses, diversified farming economies, and irrigation agriculture were of great importance. Most archaeologists also agree that urban life and pre-industrial civilization came into being gradually, during a period of major economic and social change. We can be sure that there was certainly not one overriding cause of state formation, such as irrigation, long-distance trade, or warfare.

Environmental factors were certainly major players in the complex processes of cultural change and response. In recent years, the emphasis has shifted toward a greater concern with individuals and groups. Archaeologist Norman Yoffee looks at power in three dimensions—economic, social and ideological, and political power. Each of these domains was closely linked even if one looks at them separately when doing archaeology.

Economic power depended on creating more specialized production and organizing the diverse tasks of storage and food distribution. In time, stored wealth in food and goods turned into relationships of dependency between those who produced or acquired the wealth (commoners) and those who controlled and distributed it (the elite). The latter also provided security and controlled long-distance trade networks that imported commodities not available locally, such as, for example, the gold and ivory that Egypt obtained from Nubia further up the Nile.

Social power meant ideological power, which came from compelling symbols of common cultural and political interest. These common ideologies, reinforced in private and public rituals, in art, architecture, and literature, linked individuals and their wider communities with common ties that differed from the ancient one of kin. The guardians of ideology, and they were nothing less, were often thought of as intermediaries between the physical and spiritual worlds. Powerful ideologies, such as that of the sun god Amun in Egypt and those of the Ancient Maya were a vital component in ancient states. It was no coincidence that the cities of Teotihuacán in Mexico or Angkor Wat in Cambodia, and many others, had powerful associations with the spiritual world.

Political power depended heavily on a ruler's ability to use administrative and military expertise to impose authority throughout society. State bureaucracy and military leadership did not come from the traditional kin groups, but from outside them. This meant that most political power lay in foreign relations, defense, and waging war. It also played an important role in resolving major disputes between important factions at the state level in societies that were riddled with factionalism, quarrels, and rivalries. On the domestic side, significant clout still lay in the hands of local community and kin leaders. They presided over disputes revolving around land ownership and family law.

Yoffee argues that the constant interaction between these sources of power led to the emergence of new institutions—to supreme rulers and states. The political entities functioned and changed all the time. Some collapsed, others survived for generations, even centuries, but volatility was always in the background.

If Yoffee is correct, then merging states evolved in very different ways. This was because of diverse constraints, like, for example, a lack of reliable cereal crops or domesticated animals, or the ability to store food on a large scale. Many societies flourished under powerful chieftains, who were often kin leaders. Here, social inequality came from within the kin system. One can never call them inferior, for they were an alternative to the state.

Every state had a fragile, volatile relationship with its environment. Our challenge is to dissect this relationship, one governed by often complex cultural, political, and social factors.

The accounts of pre-industrial states that follow both in this chapter, and in later ones, are short narratives, based on wide diversity of sources. They are, and always will be, incomplete, for our knowledge of early civilizations is always changing, sometimes radically.

THE FIRST MESOPOTAMIAN CITIES

Marduk, king of the gods, lord of justice, farming, and thunderstorms, presided over the primordial cosmos between the Tigris and Euphrates. He mounted his storm chariot and forged order from chaos. The charismatic deity produced a land of climatic extremes of heat and chilling temperatures—Mesopotamia (Greek: "The Land Between the Rivers"). His fellow gods created the cities that vied for power in this violent land. The first was Eridu, whose earliest shrine dates to about 5500 BCE, said to have been founded by the god Enki, lord of the earth and god of wisdom, mischief, magic, crafts and creation. Two thousand years later, Mesopotamia became a patchwork of small city-states, the earliest in the world (Figure 8.1).

Mesopotamia is a hot, low-lying landscape of inhospitable sand, swamp, and dry mud flats that lies between the Tigris and Euphrates rivers in what is now Iraq. It covers the delta regions and floodplain that form a crescent shape, bordered by the Arabian and Syrian deserts to the west, and the Iranian uplands to the east. Long, intensely hot summers and harsh, cold winters would make this a desert, were it not for the two rivers. Rainfall is irregular and insufficient for growing crops. However, with human-made irrigation, the alluvial soils of the plains could be farmed and their natural fertility unlocked. Everything depended on the annual floods of the great rivers, which allowed ancient farmers to achieve high crop yields from relatively small areas of land. This enabled them to feed relatively dense populations.

By 6500 BCE, hundreds of small farming villages dotted the rolling plains of northern Mesopotamia. Quite when agriculture took hold in the low-lying south is a matter of debate, but it was either brought by migrants from the north, or began when the gradually drying climate made fishing and foraging in the swampy lowlands

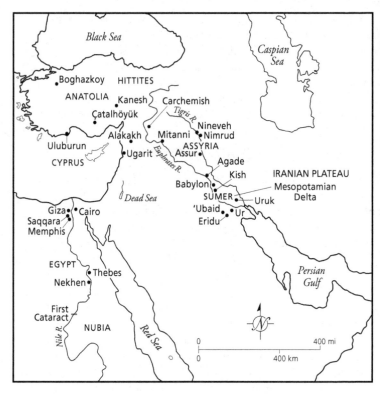

Figure 8.1 Major sites in Mesopotamia and Egypt.

near the Gulf a challenge. Whatever their origins, little groups of farming villages lay along Euphrates river channels by 6000 BCE. Five centuries later, some of these clustered communities were diverting water onto their fields, then draining it away to prevent salt accumulation. They morphed into small rural communities located around larger settlements that could have had as many as between 2500 and 4000 inhabitants.

Thus was born the 'Ubaid culture, named after a village near the ancient city of Ur. Each cluster was a group of villages linked by kin ties. Most people dwelt in humble mud-brick and reed huts, but there were more substantial buildings in larger settlements, separated by narrow alleys. From the beginning, anyone farming with river water had to depend on others. The labor involved in digging and clearing even small canals required communal effort. As more efficient ways of producing food came into being, so food surpluses grew, and social changes took hold. Sedentary settlement became commonplace; population densities increased; dominant groups in societies became more active in farming and trade. These changes occurred over a wide area and far upstream along the rivers.

As Mesopotamian society became more complex in the centuries that followed, so a need arose for more centralized authority. In time, small village ceremonial centers appeared, much larger communities developed, and the world's first cities came into being. The earliest, Eridu, had perhaps 5,000 inhabitants, and lay amidst a fertile riverside landscape, now desert, where the city mound lies. Excavations have revealed at least five stratified mud-brick temples and ten shrines at the same location, the earliest dating to about 4500 BCE. The offering table still carried hundreds of sea perch bones, offerings from the shallow estuaries nearby.

Another large settlement, Uruk, began life as a small town and soon became a growing city. During the fourth millennium BCE, it grew to an estimated 250 hectares, with satellite villages extending out about 10 kilometers. All provided fish, grain, or meat for the growing city population. The city itself was a jigsaw of neighborhoods shared by fellow kin or artisans, narrow alleyways, and courtyards. High overhead, the stepped temple mound, or ziggurat towered over the lowlands for miles around (Figure 8.2). The ziggurat and its satellite temples were the center of Uruk life, serving not only as places of worship but as storehouses, workshops, and centers of government.

The ruler of Uruk was both a secular and spiritual ruler of a complex, growing hierarchy of minor officials, wealthy landowners, and merchants. Under them were thousands of commoners: fishers, farmers, sailors, and slaves. By 3500 BCE, Uruk and other cities had developed elaborate management systems. Two important innovations now appeared. The first was metallurgy with copper being imported from the Iranian highlands. At first, it was valued for shiny ornaments, but the advent of lead and tin after 2000 BCE brought tougher-edged bronze tools and weapons.

The second innovation was writing, whose origins went back far into the past, first developed as a way of tracking inter-village

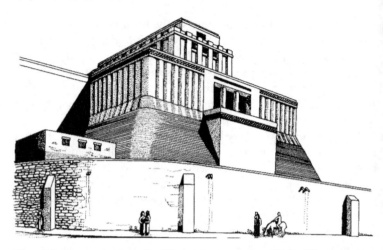

Figure 8.2 Reconstruction of an Uruk culture temple at Eridu. The great platform supports the temple. Note the drainage pipes in the walls.

shipments. The villagers may have used stringed clay tokens as early
as 8000 BCE, but by 5000 BCE, there were endless possibilities for
accounting errors and theft. Some clever officials made small clay
tablets and scratched them with incised signs that depicted familiar
items such as animals. From there it was a short step to simplified,
more conventional cuneiform (Greek: *cuneus*, wedge), with its
wedge shaped signs.

This was when scribes came into play: specially trained individuals
who compiled lists and inventories for day-to-day trade. Eventually,
the more creative among them explored the limitless opportunities
to express themselves. Rulers used tablets to trumpet their victories;
fathers chided their errant sons. Later Sumerian literature includes
epics, love stories, hymns to the gods, and tragic laments.

THE SUMERIANS (C. 3100–2334 BCE)

By 3100 BCE, Sumerian civilization was in full swing. This was
a new human experience during centuries when long-distance
trade and exchange mushroomed. A rapidly developing economic
system linked hundreds of Southwest Asian societies, all the way

from eastern Iran and the Indus Valley in Pakistan to Mesopotamia, the eastern Mediterranean, and the Nile Valley. All of this developed as a result of insatiable demands for non-local raw materials in different ecological regions where societies were developing greater complexity. Sumer was a treeless environment with fertile soils, but no metals, little timber, and no semi-precious stones. They obtained these commodities by trading bulk cargoes, like grain, along the rivers. Well-organized caravans of pack animals linked Anatolia and the Iranian highlands to the Euphrates, and the Sumerian heartland to growing, eastern Mediterranean cities. By 3000 BCE, long-term interdependency was a vital reality for Southwest Asian states.

Sumerian civilization was a volatile tapestry of political alliances and individual obligations of friendship that linked community with community, and a patchwork of what were now city-states. This was a fractious, volatile world, governed by highly competitive, often militaristic, rulers. As the Mesopotamian delta became an increasingly human-controlled environment and long-distance trade intensified, so competition for resources of all kinds intensified. Clay tablets tell of warfare and constant bickering between neighbors. Each city-state raised an army to defend its water rights, trade routes, and city walls. Despotic kings assumed power, supposedly appointed by the gods. City-states like Kish, Uruk, and Ur enjoyed periods of political strength and prosperity. Then, just as abruptly, the tide of their fortunes changed, and they sank into obscurity.

Some Sumerian leaders entertained far bolder visions than merely presiding over a few city-states in the delta. In about 2400 BCE a monarch of Ur named Lugalzagesi boasted that he ruled over a huge area from the Gulf to the Mediterranean. He did nothing of the sort. Sumerian cities did dominate overland trade routes between Mesopotamia, Turkey, and the Mediterranean coast, but their control was probably illusory. Over many centuries, however, the greatest rivalry surrounded control of Mediterranean coastal cities. Here two oceans and three continents meet; there were no natural harbors, so control of overland trade routes was the key to dominating a vast area of the known world, including resource-rich Anatolia, and grain-rich Egypt.

AKKADIANS (2334 TO 1650 BCE)

The constant back-and-forth between cities and states waxed and waned in regions surrounding Sumer, the Sumerian homeland. Inevitably, some leaders came to power with much wider ambitions. In the 24th to 32rd centuries BCE, Akkadian cities upstream came under a Semitic-speaking leader, Sargon. He founded a ruling dynasty at Akkad near Babylon in 2334 BCE. Skillful commercial ventures and carefully organized military campaigns enabled him to establish loose control over both Sumer and northern Mesopotamia. At first Akkad prospered, but it became heavily dependent on grain from the north. Cave deposits from a cave in northern Iran record two long droughts, especially one in 2260 BCE, which endured for 290 years. Starving farmers flocked to the south, where the rulers of Ur constructed a 180-kilometer long wall called "Repeller of Amorites" (herders). Akkad collapsed after years of bitter conflict.

Fifty years of political instability followed before King Ur-Nammu of Ur took control of Sumer and Akkad in 2112 BCE. He forged a kingdom that extended far to the north. Tablets from royal archives tell us that Ur-Nammu and his successors placed great emphasis on consolidating their domains into a well-organized bureaucracy.

Regardless of political shifts and occasional warfare, the economic interdependence between different regions of Southwest Asia persisted. Desert caravans and heavily laden ships were a symbol of a more durable world system that transcended the boundaries of local states and even entire civilizations. The strategic eastern Mediterranean coast lay at the heart of this vast and ever-changing system.

Three great kingdoms now cast a shadow over the eastern Mediterranean coast. Egypt lay to the south (see Chapter 9), Mitanni to the east of the Euphrates, and Hatti (the kingdom of the Hittites) in Anatolia. Their dealings were a diplomatic and political maze. They competed directly in the coastal zone, while engaged in complex dealings on their frontiers. A priceless archive of diplomatic correspondence from Amarna in Egypt records some of the intricate gifting and diplomatic maneuvering between the pharaoh and the rulers of Mitanni. The pharaoh Amenhotep III married the Mitanni ruler Tushratta's daughter in the early fourteenth century BCE. She entered the pharaoh's harem as one of his many wives. Diplomatic marriages were a powerful currency of the day.

THE HITTITES (BEFORE 1650 TO 1200 BCE)

The Hittites, based at Kanesh in Anatolia, were the newest and arguably the most able diplomatic players. They expanded their domains before 1650 BCE and seized control of the rest of Anatolia. This was just the beginning. Hittite kings acquired enormous power in Southwest Asia from their new capital at Boghazkoy, which was defended by 6.4 kilometers of city walls. They relied on diplomacy but, above all, on well-orchestrated military power. During the fifteenth century BCE, Egypt had turned Syria into a province of the pharaoh's domains. The Hittites (Hatti) pressed hard on the Egyptians. Eventually The Great King of Hatti, Suppiluliumas I (1375–1335 BCE) claimed Lebanon as his frontier. A peace treaty of 1269 BCE between the Egyptians and Hittites confined Egyptian influence to southern Palestine. Grandiloquent public architecture of the day depicted Egyptians and Hittites locked in battle using state-of-the art weaponry, including light chariots manned by archers.

By 1200 BCE, Hatti's strength began to wane; the Hittites had prospered because their well-organized army had stabilized a region notorious for political conflict. The Hittite kings controlled two great mercantile cities, Carchemish on the Euphrates River and Alalakh of Mukish in the west. Ugarit on the northern Levant coast was a cosmopolitan city ruled by a monarch who ruled like a merchant-prince. He controlled vast quantities of gold and a fleet of more than 150 ships, some of considerable size. The Hittites, however, were never a maritime power, which meant that Ugarit controlled trade between the Nile, Cyprus, and the Aegean Sea.

Hatti's fatal weaknesses lay in its land-based power, and also in its rigid social and political system, which centralized power in Boghazkoy. Change was near impossible. When severe drought impacted much of the eastern Mediterranean around 1200, thousands of foreigners flocked into Anatolia from the northwest. The central government collapsed as powerful vassal rulers threw off the Hittite yoke. Anatolia dissolved into dozens of small city-states, each striving to maintain its independence.

THE ULUBURUN SHIPWRECK (1310 BCE)

The volume of trade in the eastern Mediterranean was staggering. The lucrative gold, copper and pottery trade in the hands of eastern Mediterranean and Mycenaean Greek traders operated for centuries, unseen beneath the umbrella of constant political intrigue and endemic warfare.

Commerce was anonymous, so it is rare that we can decipher it. Fortunately, the wreck of the Uluburun ship on the southern Turkish coast in about 1310 BCE provides a telling portrait. The heavily laden merchant vessel was driven ashore in a squall. In an era when heavy sailing vessels were hard to maneuver in rough seas, shipwrecks were commonplace. Few sea captains left port during the stormy winter months.

Meticulous underwater excavations recovered much of the extraordinary cargo. Ten tonnes of copper ingots were aboard, each weighing about 27 kilograms. This would have equipped a small army with weapons and armor. A tonne of resin made and transported in two-handled jars by people in Syria was destined as incense for Egyptian rituals. Dozens of blue glass disks and ingots were on their way from Tyre on the Levant coast to Egypt. The cargo also included hardwood, highly prized amber from the Baltic far to the north, tortoise shells, elephant tusks, hippopotamus teeth, ostrich eggs, jars of olives, even large storage jars holding densely stacked Canaanite and Mycenaean clay vessels.

The Uluburun ship carried a truly royal cargo, which came from Egypt, the eastern Mediterranean coast, the Greek mainland, the Aegean islands, Cyprus, and even copper from Sardinia far to the west. This amazing wreck gives us a snapshot of the international trade that passed through the eastern Mediterranean during the second millennium BCE. Small wonder that the great powers of the day competed savagely for control of the eastern Mediterranean shore. The coastline lay at the very center of an interlocking maze of trade routes that spanned a vast tapestry of powerful states.

THE ASSYRIANS (1365–612 BCE)

The city of Assur on the Tigris River had long been an important center since Sumerian times. Assur's merchants traded far to the east and west, controlling trade down the Tigris to Babylon and beyond. During the reign of King Ashur-uballit (1365–1330 BCE), the city achieved great prominence under a ruthless monarch who practiced sophisticated diplomacy and efficient conquest. He maintained diplomatic relations with the Hittites and Mitanni to the west, and also with Babylon. Ashur-uballit's power came from control of the bountiful grain harvests of northern Mesopotamia, and tight control of long-distance trade routes. But his hold on conquered territories was far from strong, and his domains collapsed soon after his death.

The Assyrians were still powerful traders however, and a second imperial expansion came in the ninth century, fueled by fierce, well-organized annual military campaigns. Their rulers had become absolute despots, vain and grandiloquent men, who boasted of their conquests on their palace walls. When King Ashurnasirpal II (r. 883–859 BCE) completed his palace at Nimrud on the Tigris, he threw a party on a magnificent scale. "47,074 men and women from the length of my country" were guests, also 1,5000 royal officials and 5,000 foreign envoys. The king fed this throng of some 69,000 people by slaughtering 14,000 sheep and providing 10,000 skins of wine. This was partying on a grand scale, but very much a political event, carefully staged to impress those in attendance. The walls of the palace displayed bas reliefs that depict the king lion hunting and at war (Figure 8.3).

Everything in Assyrian palaces reminded the king's subjects of his royal magnificence at the height of the empire. The journey was not always smooth. The closing years of the life of Assurbanipal's successor, Shalmaneser III (859–824 BCE), were dominated by rebellions and revolts. Half a century of economic and cultural stagnation later, Tiglath-Pileser III (744–727 BCE) ascended the throne. Assyria was in the throes of a revolution, with civil war and pestilence devastating the country. The king's solution was to make sweeping changes to the Assyrian government and to consolidate Assyrian power more firmly than ever before. Assyrian policy was directed towards reducing the whole civilized world into a single empire, so that all trade and wealth fell into Assyrian hands. His initiatives included the invasion of Israel in 738 BCE, upon which he imposed a heavy taxation, as bitterly recorded in the Old Testament; also, the subsequent invasion of Babylonia, where he captured their king and crowned himself King of Babylon. This military expansionism continued afoot under

Figure 8.3 Imperial might. King Assurnasirpal wrestles with a lion in a grandiloquent display of royal power on the walls of his Nimrud palace.
Fierce lions were a constant hazard in the king's day, so grappling
with this menace became a symbolic display of royal power.

his successors. Indeed, the empire reached its greatest extent in 671
BCE, when King Esarhaddon (681–669 BCE) conquered Egypt,
which soon, however, slipped from his grasp.

The Assyrian empire was an enormous enterprise. The major
cities grew rapidly. King Esarhaddon completely rebuilt Babylon,
rejuvenating the area and bringing a new-found peace to the region.
His predecessor, King Sennacherib (705–681 BCE), had likewise
built a new and elaborate palace at Nineveh, upstream from Nimrud, with a hanging garden in which screw pumps caused water
to cascade down channels and ornamental cascades. At its height
Nineveh covered 750 hectares.

Roads linked administrative centers, which may sometimes be
traced on satellite images of northern Mesopotamia. Assyrian farmers
labored on large-scale irrigation works, building canals and dams to
enhance the productivity of the land. Rulers boasted of their ability

to control and divert river and stream water, using irrigation systems that diverted water to hitherto unusable land. They deported entire populations from conquered lands to increase productivity in newly colonized areas. All of this was far more than an effort to control a pre-existing agricultural landscape. It was an attempt to reorganize entire landscapes through massive investments in infrastructure and arbitrary reorganization of populations. We know this because settlement archaeology has shown that the old patterns of cities and hinterlands gave way to smaller villages and farmsteads that filled the gaps between the cities. The environmental consequences of such reorganization included massive deforestation and erosion of hillsides, with low-lying cities becoming vulnerable to flooding.

King Ashurbanipal died in 631 BCE, the moment when the Assyrian empire finally came apart. In 612 BCE, the Babylonians achieved independence, after the Babylonians and Persians sacked Nineveh. King Nebuchadnezzar II of Babylon now ruled over Mesopotamia and ruled over Mesopotamia for 43 years. He turned Babylon into a stupendous capital with a huge ziggurat and a lavish processional way. It was to Babylon that a large contingent of Jews were transported after the king's armies sacked Jerusalem. An exile immortalized by the Biblical psalmist: "By the waters of Babylon we sat down and wept" (Psalm 137:1).

Nebuchadnezzar's empire did not last long after his death in 562 BCE. His successors were weak and unable to resist the enemies that pressed upon the empire. The armies of Cyrus the Great of Persia took Babylon virtually without resistance in 556 BCE. By then, the effects of constant political instability and poor agricultural management were coming home to roost. The Mesopotamian delta had been a totally artificial environment by 200 BCE. Poor drainage and badly maintained irrigation works in later centuries led to inexorable rises in the salt content of the soil. Crop yields fell drastically in some areas. Nothing could be done to reverse the trend until modern science and irrigation methods could be imported at vast expense.

After Nebuchadnezzar, the eastern Mediterranean came under the sway of empires much larger than ever before. These were the centuries of Classical Greece, when Rome emerged as a major power, and the basic foundations of western civilization were laid. But what had begun as an adaptation to the realities of living in an arid, but fertile, floodplain environment had developed into a web of economic and political interdependency that was far larger than anything the world had seen before. Globalization was underway.

★★★

Ur, Iraq, c. 2600 BCE... A steep ramp cut into the earth leads to the stone burial chamber with its vaulted roof. Inside, a ruler lies in splendid regalia and gold helmet. Richly adorned women, also wearing elaborate headdresses, and royal guards file into the burial pit. The ladies of the court line up outside the burial chamber; two heavy four-wheeled carts drawn by three bullocks attended by drivers and grooms line up in front of the entrance. Royal guards with copper helmets and spears stand in ranks at the foot of the ramp. With swift, deadly blows, soldiers quickly kill all the victims in the pits and the beasts. Then high officials cover the dead with mats and supervise the filling of the great pit as music plays and priests utter invocations.

Leonard Woolley's notes on his excavation of the royal tombs at Ur are lost, so this is a largely speculative scenario.

FURTHER READING

The literature on the origins of states is enormous, therefore our list is incomplete. Chris Scarre, Charles Golden, and Brian Fagan, *Ancient Civilizations*, 5th ed. (Abington: Routledge, 2021), is an overall summary of pre-industrial states for beginners. Bruce Trigger, *Understanding Early Civilization: A Comparative Study* (Cambridge: Cambridge University Press, 2003) is definitive. Norman Yoffee, *Myths of the Archaic State: Evolution of the Earliest States, States, and Civilizations* (Cambridge: Cambridge University Press, 2005), is a perceptive analysis. For social and political aspects of the issue, see Kent Flannery and Joyce Marcus, *The Creation of Inequality: How our Prehistoric Ancestors set the Stage for Monarchy, Slavery, and Empire* (Cambridge, MA: Harvard University Press, 2012). Susan Pollock, *Ancient Mesopotamia* (Cambridge: Cambridge University Press, 2000), is an excellent summary, as is Nicholas Postgate, *Early Meso-potamia: Society and Economy at the Dawn of History* (London: Kegan Paul, 1992).

BY NILE AND INDUS
(C. 3100 TO 30 BCE)

EGYPT: UNIFYING THE TWO LANDS

Thebes, Egypt, c. 2025 BCE... All the soldiers were young, in the prime of life, buried in linen shrouds close to pharaoh Mentuhotep's sepulcher. The dry conditions preserved their thick mops of hair, all bobbed off square at the nape of the neck. They had died in an attack on a fort, killed by arrows shot downward from above, or by crushing blows from rocks hurled from the walls. They had sheltered in vain under their thin shields and fled out of range. Some of them were overtaken by showers of arrows. At least one fell as an arrow pierced his chest from behind. He fell forward as the reed shaft broke and then bled to death. The defenders had then sallied forth and clubbed at least a dozen wounded men to death. Waiting ravens and vultures scavenged the corpses, tearing off flesh with their beaks. A second attack was successful, for these bodies were recovered and buried with honor in a special tomb near to their king.

Egypt was a linear civilization, isolated from its neighbors by some of the harshest desert landscapes on earth, also by mountains, and the sea. The Nile, navigable for nearly 1,000 kilometers up to the First Cataract, was the highway through the pharaohs' kingdom that held everything together. Prevailing winds blowing upstream and the river current, flowing downstream carried pharaohs on their ceremonial excursions to the temples of the sun god Amun at

DOI: 10.4324/9781003177326-9

Thebes (modern-day Luxor), transported armies, busy officials, and merchants about their business.

"Egypt is the gift of the river," wrote the Greek historian Herodotus, who visited the Nile around 500 BCE. He saw that Egyptian civilization depended on *akhet*, the annual summer flood that arrived from far upstream and inundated the fertile soil. *Kmt*, "the black land," was the Nile floodplain, a green arrow that slashes northward across the eastern Sahara. From high in space, *Kmt* looks like a lotus flower with roots deep in Africa. The stalk was *Ta-shema*, Upper Egypt, about 800 kilometers long, relatively narrow and often bounded by cliffs. Far downstream, the stalk became a flower, as the river meandered through *Ta-mehu* (Lower Egypt), an 8,500-square kilometer delta that became the breadbasket and vineyard of the pharaohs. These were the "Two Lands of Ancient Egypt" that became a unified state in a triumph of order over chaos in about 3100 BCE.

But how did Ancient Egyptian civilization come into being? For many centuries, the Nile had nourished a valley hemmed in by semi-arid grasslands with enough rainfall to support cattle herders. The Saharan nomads had long visited settled farming villages by the river. Then the desert became much drier after 6000 BCE, so they moved permanently onto the floodplain, led by chiefs with long experience and exceptional ritual abilities. They brought new ideas with them, notions of leaders as strong bulls and herdsmen, and also the worship of the cow-headed goddess of fertility, Hathor. This may have created a tradition of dictatorial leadership, centered around water control. Confident, authoritarian leadership became ingrained in village society.

The valley population grew. Clusters of villages became larger settlements, then small kingdoms. Nekhen, upstream of Thebes, was venerated as the home of the powerful falcon god Horus (see map, Figure 8.1). A brilliantly colored temple honoring him stood above the huddled buildings of the town. Nekhen was the cradle of Egyptian kingship, where a cemetery for prominent individuals lay outside the town walls. We do not know their names, but they apparently ruled over Upper Egypt. In 3500 BCE, growing towns flourished along the river, some of them major craft centers, trading such commodities as finely wrought clay pots up and down the Nile. Egypt was becoming a cosmopolitan land, with connections by ship and donkey caravan to the Levant and by sporadic contact with Mesopotamia.

Inevitably, the patchwork of towns and small domains competed for trade and political advantage. Eventually, unnamed rulers from Upper Egypt unified the Two Lands, apparently by force. The first well-identified king of a unified Egypt was Horus Aha, or Menes, in about 3000 BCE. We know little about him, except that he moved his capital from Nekhen far downstream to Memphis, the city of the creator god Ptah, close to the boundary between Upper and Lower Egypt. This was the "Balance of the Two Worlds," where the pharaoh mediated between the forces of order and chaos. Not that governing the new state was straightforward: the early rulers presided over a country that was a maze of competing provinces and a million people.

The early pharaohs exercised control over their linear domain using a system of government that built on ancient networks of headmen and chiefly families. They placed members of their own families and trusted relatives, the "Followers of Horus," in high administrative positions. Loyal chieftains became appointed nomarchs, presiding over tribal territories, nomes. A small elite governed Egypt for the king, rewarded with titles, emblems of rank, and estates. The tentacles of careful administration extended from Memphis to towns and villages through the valley. This long-enduring system depended on a strong ruler. His administration relied on a literate minority—literate scribes.

SCRIBES AND *MA'AT*

Writing was power, the invention of the ibis-headed scribe god Thoth. Thus, words had a magical power, giving scribes a vital role in the state, a "fine profession." Scribes were everywhere. Their pens, palettes and papyrus-reed rolls documented and measured the harvest, the storerooms and the contents of grain bins. Scribes had access to information, to inventories, village censuses, and predicted heights of Nile floods. They had basic mathematical skills and could calculate length, area, volume and survey land. The more important among them were high officials, complete with staffs of office. Many were tax collectors in a state that thrived on information. Like the courtiers that surrounded the pharaohs, they were a class apart.

Almost all Egyptians were illiterate commoners, who lived lives of unremitting toil. Like all pre-industrial civilizations, Egypt ran not with elaborate technology, but with the labor of beasts of burden and human hands—and watercraft.

The earliest pharaohs wrestled with competing loyalties, for every nome (territorial division) had its own gods, despite the divine king. The solution lay in a powerful ideology. Each morning, the sun rose, establishing order out of the dark chaos of night. Human beings were the primary cause of unrest on earth, but the ideal was *ma'at*, "order" or "rightness," the notion that one lived in harmony with others, and also with gods. *Ma'at* governed the deeds of every Egyptian pharaoh for more than 3000 years. The pharaoh wore the regalia of a pastoral chief, an apron at his waist, his back protected by a bull's tail hanging from a belt. He carried the crook and flail of the shepherd. A double crown combined the red and white headdresses of Upper and Lower Egypt. The ideology soon went further. By 2500 BCE, the pharaoh's name appeared in an oval royal cartouche that depicted the sun circling the universe. Another one named the king the Son of Re, the sun god. The early rulers developed a long-lasting religious ideology that proclaimed they maintained order in the presence of the supreme divine force—the sun. The effect was mind-numbing—the pharaoh being both divine and infallible, a symbol of eternity.

OLD KINGDOM EGYPT (C. 2680–2180 BCE)

Around 2680 BCE, the Third Dynasty brought the first true flowering of Egyptian civilization. They used dramatic settings for their carefully staged public appearances—displays of regal power. Imhotep, the high priest of the sun god, built a unique stepped pyramid at Saqqara in Lower Egypt as a replica of the primeval earthen mound where the god Atum had emerged at the "first moment," the Creation. This was a stairway which allowed the deceased pharaoh, Djoser, to join the sun god in his solar boat at the moment when the sun's rays illuminated the summit. The pyramid towered 60 meters above the desert, surrounded by a wall with a palace-like façade that surrounded the entire mortuary complex. The court in front of the pyramid was the setting for royal appearances, complete with throne platform, and a token palace.

During Djoser's lifetime, kingship became synonymous with the sun god, his priesthood increasingly powerful. Earlier rulers lay in subterranean tombs. Now the pharaoh "went to his double … a ladder is set up for him that he may ascend on it"—a pyramid. During the centuries of the Old Kingdom, court cemeteries and pyramid complexes extended over a 35-kilometer stretch of the desert's edge, north of the royal capital at Memphis. The stepped pyramid prototype developed by trial and error into the perfect pyramidal form, which culminated in the pharaoh Khufu's Great Pyramid of Giza, built around 2580 to 2560 BCE.

By any standards, the pyramids of Giza are a stupendous achievement, constructed as they were with the simplest of technology and the labor of thousands of villagers. The Egyptians' expertise lay in their ability to organize, feed, and deploy large numbers of artisans and laborers to quarry, haul, and dress the boulders and rubble that made up the pyramids. Much of the stone arrived from upstream at a rock-cut harbor. During the flood season, when farming was at a standstill, thousands of villagers formed construction teams that transported quarried stone and finished boulders up earthen ramps around the rising pyramids. When the structure was complete, the clay ramps were removed and thrown into the Nile. An elaborate complex of worker settlements and housing for officials lay close to the pyramids. Many of the skeletons from worker's cemeteries nearby reveal telltale signs of malnutrition and work-related injuries.

The Great Pyramid of Khufu covers 5.3 hectares and is 146 meters high, the top once capped with a gilded pyramidion. Well over two million limestone blocks went into its construction. Khufu even deposited his disassembled funerary barge by this pyramid for his journey to the afterworld. His successor, Khafre, built a slightly smaller pyramid to the southwest around 2570 BCE. He also created the Sphinx, a human-headed recumbent lion, as guardian of the sacred precincts. The Giza Plateau became an elaborate mortuary complex, with causeways linking the pyramids to mortuary temples, where the god Horus wrapped his wings around the neck of the dead ruler. A third, smaller pyramid built by Menkaure, again to the southwest, was hastily constructed. It is as if the pharaohs' ambitions for pyramid building were scaled down, perhaps because the cost was so enormous.

With the pyramids and other public works, Egypt's rulers not only honored royal ancestors, but turned the state into the great provider. In a way, this was a form of unwritten social contract, where the pharaoh was a divine monarch, his person served by annual labor. Pyramids were huge public works that made the pharaoh's subjects dependent upon him.

The pharaohs of the Old Kingdom were powerful, confident rulers of a virile state governed by a privileged class of royal relatives and high officials. We know little about them, but they were, by all accounts, ruthless, even despotic, kings who maintained firm control over what was a prosperous state. The king's life was an intensely political existence, hemmed in by elaborate protocol and ritual observance. As a later Greek writer reported: "There was a set time ... even for his taking a walk, bathing, and sleeping with his wife."

The last great Old Kingdom pharaoh was Pepi II (2284–?2184 BCE), said to have ruled for a staggering ninety-four years (although the length of his reign is disputed). His immediate successors never matched his authority. As central power waned, so ambitious nomarchs gained more power. The decline in the monarchy coincided with a severe drought, which fell upon much of Africa and the Middle East in 2250 BCE. The Nile floods failed year after year. Contemporary writers refer to anarchy, famine, and drinking water shortages. Those leaders who maintained irrigation works and maintained basic food supplies, often by rationing, survived generations of short-lived pharaohs in Memphis. It was not until 2040 BCE that a prince named Mentuhotep, headquartered at Thebes in Upper Egypt, conquered his rivals in Lower Egypt and reunited the Two Lands. But unrest continued until the pharaoh Amenemhet seized power in 1991 BCE, when political stability returned to the Nile.

THE MIDDLE KINGDOM (C. 2040–1640 BCE)

A different ruling style came into being, a time when the pharaohs became slightly less remote and more human than their predecessors. Over four centuries, the Middle Kingdom rulers created a state with an elaborate, predictable bureaucracy, while establishing some loose governance over Nubia, "the Land of the Blacks", upstream of the First Cataract. The state mined copper, gold, and turquoise in the Sinai Desert and traded cedar wood from Lebanon. Meanwhile,

Figure 9.1 Egyptian farmworkers gather the harvest. An idealized painting from the tomb of Mereruka, Saqqara, *c.* 2400 BCE. The reality was much harsher.

John Elk III/Alamy Stock Photo

rulers organized massive irrigation works in the Fayum Depression west of the Nile that produced much higher crop yields (Figure 9.1). With three million people now living within their frontiers, they had no other option. This was now a society with well-defined social classes, reflected both in house design and occupations. These included priests, scribes, and soldiers, and numerous small households with relatives, widows, and small children. Social inequality was part of *ma'at*, an ordered world.

The pharaoh whose reign is regarded as the golden age of the Middle Kingdom, was Amenemhet III (ruled *c.* 1860–1814 BCE). He commissioned enormous temples during decades of significant prosperity. One, a mortuary temple attached to his pyramid at Hawara, was so impressive that the Greek historian Strabo praised it as a wonder of the world. His reign saw many Asiatics living along the Nile, not only merchants, but such specialists as winemakers. Nomadic herders came to the delta to buy grain and seek refuge from yet another prolonged drought. Inevitably, some of them acquired political influence, being known as *Hikau khasui,* "Princes of Desert Uplands" (Hyksos). They soon seized power over Lower Egypt. The Hyksos brought new ideas to the isolated land. They introduced bronze technology and traded silver from Asian mines. They brought, too, new weaponry—stronger bows, new styles of swords and daggers, and the horse-drawn chariot.

Tensions between Thebes and the Hyksos were such that conflict was inevitable. Around 1550 BCE, a Theban prince, Kamose, attacked Hyksos strongholds along the Nile. His son Ahmose chased the Hyksos out of Egypt. From this moment, Egypt became an imperial power, a major political force in the fragile balance of power in the eastern Mediterranean world.

MEANWHILE, BY THE INDUS ...

Apart from being the eastern frontier of Egypt, the Red Sea had long been a connective tissue between Mediterranean lands, the Persian Gulf and western India. Knowledgeable sailors used the monsoon winds to coast to the Gulf and beyond, where timber and spices could be obtained. Indian ships are known to have visited Red Sea ports regularly, but there are no records of direct contacts between the pharaohs and the sophisticated Indus civilization that arose in what is now Pakistan and western India.

In dramatic contrast to Egypt, here powerful monsoons brought abundant harvests. Today (at least), two different weather systems dominate: a winter cyclone and a summer monsoon. If one system fails to deliver rain then the other almost always will. Famine caused by crop failure is therefore currently unknown in the Indus Valley—but whether this was always so in the past is unclear. What we do know is that the centuries around 2550 BCE, at the height of Old Kingdom Egypt, saw strong monsoons and ample crops over a wide area of at least 800,000 square kilometers (an area roughly a quarter the size of Western Europe). A large, widely dispersed society, known to us as the Indus Civilization, developed over about six centuries after about 2550 BCE. The cultural focus lay in the Indus and (now-dried-up) Saraswati river valleys. But this remarkable society extended much further afield, over a broad range of environments from highland Baluchistan and the foothills of the Himalayas across the lowlands of Punjab and Sind to near what is now Mumbai.

This was no compact state. Well over a thousand Indus settlements lie across these ecological zones. Most were villages, but there were at least five major cities. The Indus homeland nurtured the largest urban culture of the time, twice the size of its equivalents in Egypt or Mesopotamia, supporting perhaps a million people, equivalent to Ancient Rome at its height. Major Indus cities thrived for an impressive six or seven centuries between about 2600 and 1900 BCE, during the height of Old Kingdom and most of Middle Kingdom Egypt.

The most imposing Indus cities were Harappa and Mohenjo-Daro along the Indus River Valley. There were none of the richly adorned elite palaces, temples and tombs like those found in Egypt or Mesopotamia. Nor were there boastful inscriptions or portraits of divine rulers touting their victories (Figure 9.2). The Indus cities were far from

Figure 9.2 Portrait of a man, perhaps a priest, from Mohenjo-Daro, Indus Valley.
SPE Media Pte Ltd/Alamy Stock Photo

bombastic. Citadels with carefully constructed, yet rather pragmatic, public buildings overlooked Harappa and Mohenjo-Daro, including a brick-built granary and a ceremonial bath. For all their understated architecture, the two cities were among the most sophisticated in the world of their day. They had imposing flood protection works, wells, and sanitation worthy, so the experts agree, of the modern era—including shower cubicles, and plumbed-in toilets, the earliest in the world by a thousand years or more. At each city, the builders followed an irregular plan that evolved over many generations that included grids of streets and houses.

One can think of Indus urban centers as polycentric communities with walls and platforms delineating different zones within larger and smaller settlements outside the cities, where economic activities unfolded and artisans labored. Indus civilization may have been a non-hierarchical society where communal activities were commonplace. Yes, its cities may also have been quarrelsome, as settled humans often are. But drawing attention to possible local spats is rather unfair of us, given that this is the only known pre-industrial civilization in the world with zero evidence for any organized warfare. Everything points to a society that was, at least at the city-level, peaceful, prosperous, and apparently mainly egalitarian (if one can imagine such a thing within our own capitalist world). It was well connected too, for its people traded with the Persian Gulf and Mesopotamia for many centuries. Atypically, it also lacked any of civilization's usual overt signs of religion. There are no obvious temples, no tombs dedicated to the afterlife, nor even any altars or offering tables. All we have are stamp seals with possible religious emblems, such as 'unicorns', or men seated in potential yogic poses. There is also one figurine, known to us as 'the priest-king' (although it may be neither priest nor king) that depicts a man in a robe, his eyes half-closed as though deep in meditation. Whatever kind of society flourished along the Indus and beyond, it was certainly not a social pyramid. A greater contrast with the authoritarian Egyptian and Mesopotamian states would be hard to find.

As the cities grew, so did rural settlements, many of them centered around farming, others around crafts. Many were short-lived communities; such residential instability was commonplace, especially in areas with river systems subject to frequent monsoon flooding. Indeed, family members members and kin probably spread their numbers between several settlements as an equable way of accessing water supplies. Farming practices varied widely over different areas, which would have made any form of centralized storage and control challenging, especially the feeding of large non-farming urban populations. Most likely, cities like Harappa relied on food surpluses from their immediate hinterlands, and on well-established trade networks for basic commodities, while rural villages were basically self-sufficient. No demanding lords presided over them. Here social inequality was understated, even if it lay at the core of society.

For some reason, the Indus cities dissolved around 2000 to 1900 BCE, and with them the entire civilization. We know that the south Asian summer and winter monsoons weakened around 2200 BCE, so perhaps the severe drought that descended over Africa and Asia at the time may be a partial culprit. We use the word "dissolve" on purpose, for it would be misleading to talk of collapse. There had been a long tradition of dispersal among Indus rural communities. A constant flow of people entered and left the cities, as they did smaller towns and villages. Given the close ties between villages and larger communities, which must have involved fellow kin, or at least trading partners, this is hardly surprising. Perhaps, then, the dissolution of the Indus cities may have been just a defensive response to food shortages that could be met by moving to better watered communities where food was available. After all, why provide food to a city, when you are better off looking after your own community?

The Indus Civilization thrived because it was based on a rural, social and economic underpinning that was, by its very nature, resilient and sustainable. A seemingly peaceful ideology with a lack of social hierarchy or constraining religious ideology must also have helped. Here, cities were temporary adaptations. Rural communities could endure longer-term droughts, with help from nearby communities, but certainly without the trauma experienced by hungry, dense urban populations.

EGYPT: THE NEW KINGDOM (1550–1070 BCE)

The Indus Valley civilization dissolved as Egypt became an imperial power. Pharaoh Ahmose transformed Egypt into an efficient military state, rewarding his soldiers and mercenaries with grants of land and loot, while retaining economic power and wealth in royal hands. Egypt competed with the state of Mittani, east of the Euphrates, and with the Hittites in Anatolia (modern-day Turkey). He and his successors turned Nubia into a colony and expanded trade down the Red Sea to acquire timber and "heaps of myrrh resin with myrrh trees with ebony and pure ivory".

Karnack's temple of the sun god Amun at the heart of Thebes, known as the "Estate of Amun," became a statement of raw, imperial power. Great pylons at its entrance bore brightly colored scenes of the king conquering his enemies in the presence of the gods. Here the deities found shelter and were nourished with food offerings. The priesthood of Amun and their temples were a major political force, also vital to the state's economy. Amun's temples owned vast numbers of cattle, mineral rights, and enormous grain stocks. Great pageants at Thebes, featuring formal processions between the god's temples at Karnak and Luxor, showed the populace that the pharaoh had renewed the divine *ka*, or spiritual essence, in the innermost shrine of Amun himself.

The Estate of Amun extended from the temples on the east bank of the Nile to the western bank, the domain of the dead. Starting with the Eighteenth Dynasty around 1505 BCE, the pharaoh Amenhotep and his illustrious successors chose to be buried not under conspicuous pyramids, but in secret rock-cut tombs in the arid Valley of the Kings opposite Thebes. The royal mortuary temples lay on the nearby plain, surrounded by the tombs of queens, princes, and high court officials. Generations of skilled artisans worked in the "Place of Truth," the Royal Necropolis.

Amun was all-powerful until pharaoh Akhenaten ascended the throne in 1353 BCE. He revived the ancient cult of Re-Harakhty, the primordial sun god. Akhenaten abandoned religious orthodoxy, placing great emphasis on the worship of the sun disk, the god Aten. In the fifth year of his reign, he moved his court downstream to a new capital at Amarna, a city of some 20,000 people. Amarna centered around an imposing ceremonial way that led from Akhenaten's secluded palace to Aten's temple. Most of the city's inhabitants crowded into humble dwellings. Their bodies, deposited in cemeteries outside the city, display chronic suffering from harsh labor undertaken during their brief lives.

Religious fanatic, madman, or heretic; history has rarely judged Akhenaten favorably. His 17-year reign left a corrupt and chaotic kingdom behind it. Amarna was soon abandoned; the pharaoh's successor reigned for three years, and was succeeded by eight-year-old Tutankhamun (1333–1323 BCE), an obscure ruler who achieved immortality with the discovery of his tomb, intact, by Howard Carter and Lord Carnarvon in 1922. Fortunately, he had powerful and experienced advisers, raised as they were in the old spiritual order, who restored the old spiritual order and its temples.

Tutankhamun's sudden death caught the court by surprise, but the great pharaohs of the Nineteenth Dynasty (1307–1196 BCE) restored the kingdom to its former imperial glory. Their wealth came from Nubian gold and from far-flung trade. Ramesses II (1290–1224 BCE) campaigned far into Syria. He met his match with the Hittites at the battle of Kadesh, where they fought the Egyptian army to a standstill. After this retreat, the pharaohs steadily lost political influence in the Middle East.

With the assassination of Ramesses III in 1155 BCE, Egypt entered a period of slow decline. A retreat from Nubia, setbacks in Asia, and chronic bureaucratic corruption caused the breakdown of reliable food supplies and resource management as lawlessness became endemic. The rise of Greek influence brought the Ptolemies to the throne in 305 BCE, based on Lower Egypt, always at the frontier with the outside world. In 30 BCE, after the death of the Ptolemaic dynasty's final ruler, Cleopatra VII, the land of the pharaohs became part of the Roman Empire and a major granary for distant Rome and Constantinople. Long after the great pharaohs were just memories, *akhet*, the unpredictable Nile inundation, shaped global food supplies and supported empires.

★★★

The Nile, spring, 1500 BCE... Twenty fishers caught bottom-feeding tilapia for 40 artisans working in the royal cemetery on the West Bank the Nile opposite Thebes. According to records of the day, one fisher could supply about 882 kilograms of fish over a six-month period. Along the Nile, catches were gutted, filleted, either eaten fresh or dried or pickled for later use, for fish were staple ration in Ancient Egypt. The canoes would leave at dawn, checking nets and traps set in narrow side channels, especially during the spring spawning season at the height of the flood. Some papyrus canoes set out with seine nets with support lines and tapered ends. Teams of men would haul the laden seines to shore. There, waiting scribes tallied the catches and apportioned rations. In some places, like the pyramid villages at Giza, hundreds of workers processed catches of mullet, Nile perch, and other species. As one pharaoh remarked to his son, 4000 years ago, fish were a gift from gods for humans to eat.

FURTHER READING

Toby Wilkinson, *A World Beneath the Sands: The Golden Age of Egyptology* (New York: W.W. Norton, 2020) tells the story of pioneering Egyptologists. David Wengrow, *The Archaeology of Early Egypt* (Cambridge: Cambridge University Press, 2006), is a good source on Pre-Dynastic Egypt. Toby Wilkinson's *The Rise and Fall of Ancient Egypt* (New York: Random House, 2010), is an excellent introduction, one of many volumes on the subject. Barry Kemp, *Ancient Egypt: Anatomy of a Civilization*, 3rd ed. (Abingdon: Routledge, 2017), is an authoritative description. The Indus civilization is well summarized by Andrew Robinson, *The Indus* (London: Reaktion Books, 2015). See also Jane R. McIntosh, *A Peaceful Realm* (Boulder, CO: Westview Press, 2002), and Robin Coningham and Ruth Young, *From the Indus to Asoka* (Cambridge: Cambridge University Press, 2015).

CHINA AND SOUTHEAST ASIA (AFTER 5250 BCE TO 15TH CENTURY CE)

Northern China, c. 1280 BCE... The light chariot stands atop a low ridge overlooking a shallow valley near the Huang He river. Flies swarm around the beautifully matched horses. Shang dynasty ruler Wu Ding and the driver stand motionless, feet slightly astride on the plaited-leather floor. Wu Ding raises his hand. The officers in the valley shout a command to the troops behind them, weapons at the ready. Dense clouds of dust swirl around the fierce hand-to-hand conflict, with no quarter given on either side. The ruler's warriors gain the advantage and advance over a carpet of slaughtered enemies. The chariot driver eases the horses forward closer to the fray.

Contrary to popular belief, Chinese civilization did not develop in just one place—the middle Huang He valley in the north. Only now are teams of archaeologists unraveling stories of a maze of increasingly complex farming societies that were emerging in different environments throughout China after 3500 BCE.

The earliest more complex societies arose in the Lower Yangtze Basin, where the Liangzhu culture (*c.* 3300–2200 BCE) became famous for its fine jade ornaments (Figure 10.1). Translucent jade continued to be valued throughout China until recent times, so much so that it was more valuable than gold. Small cemeteries of high-status Liangzhu individuals reveal emerging social inequality. Their ornaments hint that some of them may have been shamans.

DOI: 10.4324/9781003177326-10

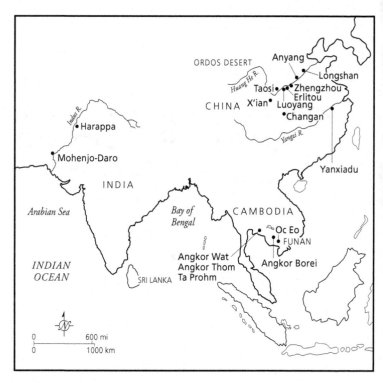

Figure 10.1 Map showing the sites mentioned in Chapter 10.

The middle Huang He river valley was the birthplace of a series of closely connected societies known collectively as the Longshan. They thrived between 2700 and 2000 BCE, the different cultures interacting vigorously with one another. Longshan potters made pottery using wheels, fine, but simple vessels fired at high temperatures in kilns hot enough to smelt and cast copper. The finest Longshan vessels were black, shiny boxes, jars, and cups that may marked the transition from clay to metal ritual vessels for the elite. Another innovation became popular—*scapulimancy*, or divination carried out by applying heated implements to animal shoulder blades and tortoise shells. The resulting cracks gave answers to questions from gods and ancestors. The earliest known Chinese script may well have originated in Longshan society.

Like Sumerian society in the west, Longshan was a culture of warring elites, who struggled to maintain their position to acquire greater power. Displaying one's power in life with ritual vessels, and after death in one's tomb, proclaimed one's social status. These were militaristic leaders, reflected in the development of rectangular defensive enclosures, built by ramming earth between timber shuttering. Some Longshan walls, constructed by large numbers of people, were up to 10 meters thick, making for durable fortifications. For example, Taosi, in southern Shanxi, is a 280-hectare rammed earth enclosure. Dividing walls separated the elite and commoners. Fifty contemporary settlements in the surrounding hinterland display three different social classes in what was a rigidly enforced social hierarchy.

XIA AND SHANG (C. 2200 TO 1046 BCE)

The traditional story of Chinese history begins with various mythical rulers, starting with the emperor-god Fuxi and his sister Nuwa, the original common ancestors of humanity. The first states emerged in today's Henan province in the middle Huang He valley. Three Xia dynasties are said to have preceded the much better known Shang, but their date is uncertain. The Xia rulers are shadowy figures, whose reigns extended from before 2000 to about 1750 BCE. During the 18th century, the Shang overthrew the Xia. In practice, however there was strong cultural continuity between the two, associated with the city of Erlitou. A 12-hectare enclosure at the center of the city featured a pair of rammed earth platforms surrounded by a substantial wall to keep out commoners. Extensive bronze-casting and turquoise workshops lay to the south, as if the production of elite objects was closely controlled.

As Shang civilization became firmly established, political power moved to Zhengzhou, 100 kilometers downstream in the heart of rich farming country. Here, a central enclosure surrounded by a tall, rammed earth fortification 7.5 kilometers long, housed the elite and ritual specialists, and also the ancient temple of the ruling lineage. An outer wall defined an area of 20 square kilometers, where bronze and pottery workshops, also cemeteries, lay. Zhengzhou, and later Anyang, may have supported large populations. But, unlike Mesopotamia or Egypt, they were ultimately ceremonial centers surrounded by subordinate villages.

The penultimate Shang capital, and the first stable one in China, was Anyang, which extended for 5.8 kilometers along the nearby Huan River. The city resembled Zhengzhou, except that there was no prominent enclosure wall. There was a ritual center, part palace, part temple, and a dispersed collection of artisans' villages and workshops. The Shang rulers of the day were intermediaries between the living and the gods and through them, the ancestors. They were ritual specialists, who were buried in a cemetery about two kilometers away. Thirteen imposing graves with ramps housed the dead, who lay in wooden chambers. One tomb had eleven rows of 59 headless sacrificial victims laid out upon its ramp. Unfortunately, looters emptied the sepulchers in ancient times.

Exactly how much territory Shang rulers controlled remains a mystery. The actual territory under their direct rule may have been small, but their cultural influence was enormous, exemplified by prestigious bronze vessels (Figure 10.2). Scapulimancy came into its

Figure 10.2 A Shang jue vessel in bronze, used for pouring wine, such vessels were symbols of prestige in Shang society.

Heritage Image Partnership Ltd/Alamy Stock Photo

own in Shang times, most surviving inscribed oracle bones coming from Anyang. The writing system invented by Xia and Shang diviners was so effective that it survived in a much modified form as the basis of modern Chinese scripts.

The oracle bones identify an inner capital and an outer domain, the former being the region around Anyang, perhaps extending 100 kilometers to the south. This was basically a feudal state, with the ruler and the royal lineage at the summit. The outer domain was probably under the control of semi-autonomous lords. They took oaths of loyalty to the Shang ruler, but still fought with one another on occasion.

The Shang was the most important early civilization in China, but it was only one of several vigorous bronze-working traditions. Shang was not the only powerful culture, merely one of several major cultural players of the day; it functioned as part of a pattern of other states with near-equal status.

ZHOU AND WARRING STATES (1046 TO 221 BCE)

The Zhou state to the west had long competed with their Shang neighbors and finally prevailed in 1046 BCE. But the cultural and technological traditions of their predecessors persisted for centuries. Zhou urban centers remained much the same until 771 BCE, when nomad raiders from the north forced the Zhou elite to move east to Luoyang. The Western Zhou remained very much a continuation of Shang, but the Eastern Zhou experienced major changes, including compact cities, coinage, iron technology, and markets. An ever-changing tapestry of competing states of different sizes rose and fell, as competition intensified between local rulers.

Eighth-century Eastern Zhou cities covered large areas, fortified by rammed earth walls. However, relatively few people dwelt in them, living in different sectors nearby, where cemeteries could also be found. Within three centuries, everything had changed. Cities were much larger, the biggest, Xiadu, housing as many as 316,000 people within its imposing walls. State capitals covered areas as large as 20 square kilometers. Their palaces lay on rammed earth platforms either within or just outside the walls. The commoners lived in poverty behind the main walls. The distance between elite and commoner was carefully calculated and added to the mystique surrounding the ruling elite.

A revolution in Chinese life was under way. The now imposing cities were far more than ceremonial centers, they were important commercial and manufacturing centers. Some cities had mints for coinage, also jade and bone workshops. By the 5th century, large iron foundries abounded. These may have provided iron tools for the farmers, thereby developing a relationship of mutual interdependence between the countryside and the cities.

Iron technology assumed ever greater importance in Chinese life, as production of iron tools and weapons accelerated. Mass production of iron was common to all major cities. Competing Eastern Zhou states could now increase agricultural production and accumulate much larger food surpluses to feed growing populations. They were also able to support ever-larger armies.

The authority of Zhou rulers was often little more than nominal. Day-to-day power lay in the hands of more than sixty states, of varying sizes, which led to centuries of small-scale warfare. A great deal of the campaigning revolved around the number of chariots that each side could bring to battle.

Then came the so-called Warring States period (Zhanguo Shidai), which began around 481 BCE. By that time, warfare was changing profoundly, with only 22 independent kingdoms still remaining. Armies now numbered in the thousands and mass-produced iron weapons led to enormous numbers of casualties in large, set-piece battles. Fighting became endemic to the point that there were large annual wars between the late 6th and early 3rd centuries. The change resulted in the abandonment of the chariot, replaced by aggressive cavalry charges and mass attacks by closely packed infantry regiments. By the 4th century, the crossbow, with its lethal, fast-moving arrows, had come into widespread use.

The violence was so catastrophic that states began to wall in their domains, the crossbow being a very effective weapon against besiegers. Such fortifications, often made of rammed earth, extended over hundreds of kilometers and required the forced labor of thousands of commoners to build. The gates were carefully guarded, controlled movement, and were a device for raising tolls. Descendants of these walls formed part of the celebrated Great Wall in later centuries.

All these walls were ineffective, to the point that only seven states survived in an era of relentless competition and ever tighter bureaucratic control. Their rulers presided over what can only be called huge killing machines. The era of endless bloodshed ended when a ruler of the Qin state defeated his major rival, Zhao. The campaign resulted in the slaughter of 400,000 prisoners. His successor built on his success and conquered Zhou and five other states. With ruthless determination, he brought all his competitors under his rule. In 221 BCE, he proclaimed himself Qin Shihuangdi, "First Emperor" of a unified China.

EMPEROR SHIHUANGDI (259–210 BCE)

Shihuangdi's success depended on his battle-tested army and also on far-reaching bureaucratic and administrative reforms. He began by dividing the kingdom into a series of provinces, each governed by officials who were answerable to him. Each was a commandery, part of a centralized imperial administration that replaced previous arrangements where defeated states survived under subject lords. Shihuangdi's state depended on 103 commanderies and numerous counties, tightly controlled by the imperial administration. At the same time, the emperor ordered the destruction of all political books and histories, except those of his Qin ancestors. He aimed to eliminate any rivals and to create a unified state ideology, dismembering any memory of earlier kingdoms. Aztec rulers in Mexico followed the same policy many centuries later, creating a myth of Aztec dominance, with considerable success (see Chapter 11).

The emperor took draconian steps to consolidate his empire. Thousands of people labored on a road network that radiated from the imperial capital, complete with posting stations and efficient guards. The rammed earth highways were 15 meters wide and even crossed extreme terrain. In the north, Shihuangdi built a Great Wall, mainly of rammed earth, which extended over 4,000 kilometers from the Korean boundary to the Ordos Desert in the west. Much of Shihuangdi's wall consisted of earlier wall segments joined into a single entity. (This should not be confused with the Great Wall of the 16th century CE, built to defend China from the Mongolians.)

The first emperor was a paranoid, superstitious tyrant, so unpopular that his dynasty did not survive long after his death in 210 BCE.

Only four years later, his capital fell to a rebel army and the new Han Dynasty took control and ruled for four centuries.

Not that the Chinese were allowed to forget their first emperor. He began construction of his sepulcher soon after the end of the Warring States and his son completed it long after his death, duly slaughtering the craftspeople who knew its secrets. The 50-meter high burial mound lies 40 kilometers east of the modern-day city of X'ian. Two huge rectangular enclosures surround an area of 2 square kilometers. Thirty to forty meters underground stands a palace, the home of the emperor in the afterlife. Later historians claim that a replica of the royal domains lies under the mound, with major rivers delineated in mercury. Scale models of palaces and pavilions contain his personal possessions and models of courtiers. Numerous sacrificial concubines were buried inside the sepulcher. More than 700,000 conscripts are said to have worked on the burial mound and surrounding park. The tomb has not been excavated. Chinese archaeologists consider that they lack the expertise and resources to excavate it to the highest scientific standards. (They are right, for no one in the world could yet carry this off.)

Qin Shihuangdi's burial mound lies in the midst of a large funerary park, protected by regiments of brightly painted terracotta soldiers, including 1,400 men and horses, infantry detachments, cavalry, and a command and control unit where the commander-in-chief is surrounded by sixty-four officers and a bodyguard selected for their height. There are underground stables near the great mound, where horses were buried alive, along with two half-scale bronze chariots and their horses. It will take years to excavate and conserve the regiments and everything else in the funerary park. If the burial mound is ever excavated, the investigation would take years.

The rulers of the Han Dynasty took over Shihuangdi's government and newly created infrastructure. Most Han subjects were subsistence farmers, but there were major cities. The capital, Changan near the Wei River, had quarter of a million inhabitants, living in a rectangular grid protected by rammed earth walls. There were twelve gates and an imperial pleasure garden. By this time, wealthy families lived in multi-storied houses, they dressed in silk and furs, and traveled in horse-drawn carriages. Meanwhile, commoners lived in dwellings said to be crammed together "as closely as the teeth of a comb." The Han ruled over China for over four centuries (202 BCE–220 CE).

By Roman times in the west, Chinese civilization had flourished for more than 2,000 years. This distinctive and highly militaristic culture was adept at assimilating conquerors and the conquered into its own traditions. In contrast, the Roman Empire came into being on the backs of slaves and collapsed when attacked by barbarian nomads. It is worth noting that much of the fabric of Chinese civilizations persists to this day.

SOUTHEAST ASIA: THE RISE OF ANGKOR (LATE FIRST MILLENNIUM BCE TO 802 CE)

By the end of the first millennium BCE, some Southeast Asian societies were showing signs of developing into highly ranked, centralized kingdoms. Their overlords formed an aristocratic class, who came to power by virtue of their close relationships with their ancestors. This was a classic form of pre-industrial governance, reinforced here by elaborate formal display, feasting, and public rituals. The increasing complexity came about in part from the expertise of their overlords at attracting loyal followers, as well as controlling trade, increasing production, and organizing labor for the common good.

All this worked well at the local level, yet inevitably, rivalries arose. Some rulers aspired to even greater status, which led them to preside over larger kingdoms carved out by force and the creation of magnificent palaces and temples, which served as the focus for elaborate public ceremonials that honored them. The leaders of such emerging states derived much of their authority by their charisma and decisive leadership.

These domains existed in a constant state of political flux with no fixed boundaries. Everything revolved around the overlords, whose abilities to cement alliances and deal with potential enemies dictated their relationships with their rivals. Some experts describe the relationships between these rulers as a *mandala*. This Sanskrit word is a political doctrine, which describes territories as circles that expand and contract according to political circumstances. Each society focused on its own center and its ruler and his retinue. The personal and spiritual qualities of the lord were an important variable in a complex, ever-changing political equation.

The emerging kingdoms flourished in fertile lowland and river-side areas, where rice agriculture flourished and fish were abundant. Dense populations occupied the lower and middle Mekong Valley, the latter including the famous Tonle Sap lake and plains, the home-land of Khmer-speaking peoples.

Chinese records refer to the lower Mekong as Funan, which meant "the port of a thousand rivers." Here prosperous trading ports in the Mekong delta traded bronze, silver, spices, and even horses brought by sea from Central Asia. Systematic drainage and waterborne trans-port transformed the delta's swamps into fertile agricultural land. Most Funanese lived in large lake cities fortified with earthworks and moats swarming with crocodiles. Oc Eo was such a port, con-nected to the ocean and linked to Funan's capital, Angkor Borei.

Between the 3rd and 6th centuries CE, the coastal region pros-pered greatly, thanks to long traditions of indigenous metallurgy and other crafts and products carried by expert traders. By the 6th century, however, the center of economic and political gravity had shifted inland to the middle Mekong and the fertile Tonle Sap. The Chinese called this area Zhenla, a region where competing overlords touted themselves as divine kings on earth. They used the Hindu god Shiva as divine justification for kingship, and to attract loyal fol-lowers. The various states behaved like a concertina, expanding and contracting as competing rulers tried to establish authority over as large an area as possible.

JAYAVARMAN II, SURYAVARMAN II, AND ANGKOR WAT (802 TO 1181 CE)

The chronic fragmentation continued until 802 CE, when a dynamic Khmer monarch, Jayavarman II, came to power. He conquered his rivals from his base near the Mekong River and set up the defeated territories as tribute kingdoms, governed by his loyal generals. Jaya-varman was a brilliant political operator. He merged the cult of the ancestors with that of Shiva to consolidate his new kingdom. His subjects were taught to worship him as a god. All the resources of an increasingly centralized government were devoted to the preserva-tion of the cult of the god-king. Everyone, whether noble, priest, or commoner, was expected to subordinate his or her ambitions to the needs of the god-king on earth, a deity in this life and the next.

Jayavarman ruled for a remarkable 45 years. He promoted himself as the incarnation of Shiva on earth, the *varman*, the protector. The king presided over an energetic bureaucracy of high-status families, which included both generals, civilian administrators, and a disciplined hierarchy of priests. Officialdom pervaded every aspect of Khmer life, from agriculture to tax collection, warfare to ritual. As was the case with every pre-industrial state, sustainability depended on large food surpluses, and the control of the enormous labor forces that constructed temples, reservoirs, canals, and other public works.

The hub of the Khmer world is known today as Angkor. Many of the thirty monarchs who followed Jayavarman II built imposing temples and artificial mounds to house the royal lingam of the king, a pillar-like symbol of Shiva, that served as mausoleums when they themselves joined the gods. The civilization that emerged was far from austere, for the Khmer carried the cult of wealth, luxury and divine monarchy to its limits. The cult reached its peak during the reign of Suryavarman II, who built Angkor Wat in the 12th century.

Suryavarman came to the throne in 1113. Soon after, he started building his masterpiece, Angkor Wat (Khmer for "Temple city"). The largest religious structure in the world, it stretches across more than 160 hectares (Figure 10.3). This extraordinary temple complex makes even the largest Sumerian ziggurat look like a village shrine. The word stupendous is an understatement. Every detail represents part of the heavenly world in a terrestrial form. The Khmer believed that the world consisted of a central continent, Jambudvipa, with the cosmic mountain, Meru, rising from its center. The gods lived at the mountain's summit, represented at Angkor Wat by the highest tower. The remaining four towers represent Meru's lesser peaks, while the enclosure wall depicts the mountains at the edge of the world, and the surrounding moat, the ocean beyond. This was the Khmers' attempt to create a monument to the Hindu god Vishnu, preserver of the universe.

Angkor Wat's central temple rises more than 60 meters above the surrounding forest, adorned with bas-reliefs that depict the monarch sitting on a wooden throne while high officials declare their loyalty to him. Nearby, the king progresses down a hillside on an elephant, accompanied by the high priest and his generals. The court rides with him through a forest, the noblewomen riding in

Figure 10.3 Angkor Wat from the air.

R.M. Nunes/Alamy Stock Photo

litters. Heavily armored soldiers defend the royal party. Battle scenes and bas-reliefs of celestial maidens appear throughout the site. The dancers wear skirts of ornate fabric, their flowered backgrounds and subtle gestures promising heavenly delights to the king upon his death. Timely inscriptions spell out the terrible punishments that await evil-doers. Suryavarman used Angkor Wat as the place where he, as divine monarch, communicated with the gods. When he died, his remains lay in the central tower, so that his soul could enter his divine image and make contact with his royal ancestors. This was when he acquired immortality and became one with Vishnu.

ANGKOR THOM AND DISSOLUTION (1181 TO THE 15TH CENTURY CE)

Building Angkor Wat was a severe drain on the kingdom's resources at a time when the king was fighting his neighbors. In 1181, a successor, Jayavarman VII, who was a Buddhist, started building a huge new capital nearby. Vast military parades and carefully orchestrated groups engaged in elaborate ceremonies and games in the Great

Plaza, which was encircle by a 12.8-kilometer wall, the ruler's funerary temple situated in the middle.

It is said that a million people lived in or near Angkor Thom (Khmer for "Great City"). The wealth lavished on public buildings, to say nothing of conscripted labor, was staggering. To give but one example, the Ta Prohm temple, dedicated to the king's mother, bears an inscription that proclaims that 306,372 people from 13,500 villages worked for the shrine. They consumed 3,000 tons of rice annually; 66,625 men and women served the gods at Ta Prohm, including 615 female dancers and 18 senior priests. Jayavarman's building projects, which included hospitals and pilgrims' shelters, were built to earn merit for the ruler and his most ardent followers. His building activities created a religious utopia where everything flowed to its center. Every product, every person's labor, and every thought aimed to embellish the hub of the universe and the kings who enjoyed it.

The prosperity and stability were an illusion. The king sat at the center of the *mandala*, a circle defined only by the loyalties of the aristocrats who ruled the outlying provinces. A Khmer ruler's power depended on his control of the center, and on his ability to provide the huge rice surpluses required to feed his subjects. This meant that most of his power depended on his ability to deliver water for rice cultivation from the Mekong River. This was a formidable task, given that Angkor's rural-urban sprawl extended over a least 1000 square kilometers and supported between 750,000 and a million people. LiDAR surveys from helicopters and space have stripped away today's forest cover and revealed that Angkor Thom alone had half a million people living in outlying communities as much as 15 kilometers from the center.

Everything ultimately depended on water management, on *barays*—the huge rectangular reservoirs that stored or drained the water that swelled the Tonle Sap lake during the annual Mekong flood. The labor required to construct and maintain this water control system was enormous, created to reduce the risks associated with variable monsoon rainfall. The canals, reservoirs, and dams were designed to ensure that the rice fields of southern Angkor produced high crop yields. The system worked well until the late 12th century, when an orgy of temple building and rising population densities overstressed the long-term strategy of simply clearing agricultural land and expanding canal networks.

At first, the Khmer water system could handle periodic droughts, but it became increasingly vulnerable, as major climatic instability affected Southeast Asia during the 13th and 14th centuries. There were cycles of serious water shortages, also major monsoon floods, both of which caused the long-established water networks to fracture. The infrastructure was centuries old; sustainability faltered; the damaged fields could no longer support the ever increasing population. No longer did the state's rulers and high officials have the ability, or the power, to recruit labor for major engineering works to fix the system.

By the mid-15th century, Angkor was largely uninhabitable. The elite left early, taking their wealth with them. This was also a time of profound political and economic change. New Buddhist doctrines de-emphasized the old practice of supporting elaborate temples, whose political influenced had declined sharply. During a period of transition, Khmer leadership and many elite families moved downstream away from the human-made Tonle Sap landscape to the lower reaches of the great river, where they depended on the annual flood. Large urban areas with their dispersed cities dissolved and smaller, compact settlements flourished on the peripheries of the once-prosperous hinterlands.

Wider economic and political development were also afoot. By the time of Christ, the monsoon winds had linked India and the Indian Ocean island of Sri Lanka with the insatiable demands of Rome for fine textiles, ivory, and spices. As trade routes connecting Asia with a much wider world expanded, so Southeast Asia's coastal cities had assumed greater economic clout. Trade inland with Angkor weakened; maritime trade with Arab, Indian, Chinese, and other seafaring entities increased. The Khmer empire faded into relative obscurity as depopulation accelerated. Once again, the inexorable forces of nascent globalization came into play.

★★★

Angkor Thom, Cambodia, c. 1296 CE... The crowds gather at daybreak in the Great Plaza, jammed tightly together in sight of the golden towers of the Bayon, the central temple. Today, the king is to appear in public. Everyone falls silent as soldiers file past, followed by banners and musicians. Gaily decorated palace girls swirl and dance, followed by the king's bodyguard, armed to the teeth, along with horse-drawn chariots. A regiment of closely massed elephants marches in attendance. Then the ruler appears, standing atop an elephant with gold-sheathed tusks, holding the sacred sword. As the monarch passes, everyone kneels and touches the earth with their foreheads under the watchful eyes of the parade marshals.

FURTHER READING

Li Feng, *Early China: A Social and Cultural History* (Cambridge: Cambridge University Press, 2013), provides an up-to-date account of early Chinese state formation from before the Shang to the Han Dynasty. Li Liu and Xingcan Chen, *Archaeology of China from the Paleolithic to the Early Bronze Age* (Cambridge: Cambridge University Press, 2012), is also authoritative. They provide comprehensive bibliographies for additional reading. C.E.W Higham, *The Origins of the Civilization of Angkor* (London: Bloomsbury 2012), and the same author's *Early Mainland Southeast Asia from the First Humans to Angkor* (Bangkok: River Books, 2014), are excellent introductions. His *Civilization of Angkor* (London: Weidenfeld & Nicholson, 2001) also provides a useful survey.

MESOAMERICA
(C. 1500 BCE TO 1532 CE)

Teotihuacán, Valley of Mexico, c. 400 CE... Walking down a narrow street, the bare, stuccoed walls of the residential compounds close in on either side. The alley is a mix of sounds and smells—barking dogs, the scent of wood smoke, the monotonous sound of maize grinding, women talking softly as they weave. Incense hangs in the air; cooking smells assault the senses along with the smell of rotting garbage. A door open to the street offers a glimpse of a shady courtyard, where newly fired clay vessels and textiles dry in the sun. Three family groups dwell in this compound, each with their own apartment. But everyone knows people in the crowded urban precinct, where an upward glance reveals the huge mass of the Pyramid of the Sun.

Mesoamerica encompasses the large area of Central America where indigenous states flourished. These kingdoms were remarkable for their elaborate religious beliefs and ceremonial rites, including human sacrifice, for their spectacular architecture of temples, plazas, and pyramids, and for their scripts and calendars. Volatile, sophisticated, and sometimes ardently militaristic, Mesoamerican civilizations developed over 3,000 years before the arrival of Spanish conquistadors in the early 16th century CE.

Two great mountain chains form the backbone of highland Mesoamerica. The inland basin of the Valley of Mexico with its five

DOI: 10.4324/9781003177326-11

lakes was the center of political and economic life at higher elevations. To the northeast, the highland mountains give way to the
Gulf Coast and the low-lying limestone peninsula of the Yucatán,
often called the Maya lowlands. The contrast between elevations
meant that Mesoamerican civilizations were always dependent on
neighbors near and far. Every society relied on constant interactions,
exchanges of ideas and commodities between people living in dramatically contrasting environments.

By 2000 BCE, maize and bean agriculture supported numerous small communities in the valleys of Mexico and Oaxaca in the
highlands and many parts of the lowlands. Over the following millennium, the first signs of political and social complexity appeared in
small chiefdoms. This was the same process that took place in Mesopotamia, Egypt, China, and elsewhere. Small shrines came into use;
trade in exotics, like stingray spines used in bloodletting ceremonies,
and sea shells took hold, objects that symbolized and legitimized the
authority of leaders to control both people and natural resources.
This period is often referred to as the Preclassic.

THE OLMEC (C. 1500 TO 400 BCE)

The best known of these societies are the Olmec, who assumed a
revered place in the legends and lore of later Mesoamerican civilizations (Figure 11.1). Olmec people lived along the Gulf Coast by
1500 BCE until around 400 CE. They formed a series of chiefdoms
along the hot and humid Gulf Coast with its fertile soils and varied
wildlife. An early Olmec community flourished at San Lorenzo by
1250 BCE, in the midst of frequently inundated woodland plains.
Soon San Lorenzo's leaders erected platforms and earthen mounds.
A century later, imposing monumental carvings adorned the site,
apparently portraits of its rulers. By the time of its decline, after 900
CE, San Lorenzo was engaged in obsidian and semiprecious stone
trade over an enormous area.

The most famous Olmec site, La Venta near the Gulf of Mexico,
took its place. Located on a small island in a swamp, La Venta's rulers
erected a rectangular earthen mound 32 meters high, surrounding it
with low mounds and a plaza. Large stone portraits, perhaps of rulers, some with savage expressions, litter the site. Throne-like blocks
display a seated figure, perhaps a ruler, emerging from a deep niche

Figure 11.1 Mesoamerica, showing the sites mentioned in Chapter 11.

carved into the stone. The sides of these altars bear stylized depictions of half-humans, half-jaguars. Jaguars were part of a complex symbolism, long associated with rain, fertility, and shamans. Such individuals could pass effortlessly from the living world into the spiritual realm and back again.

Olmec lords grafted the ancient ideology of the warrior jaguar onto an emerging institution of kingship, where the ruler was a shaman-king with awesome supernatural powers. Their artists turned eagle's fathers and claws into serpents and other beasts to form mythical creatures such as the "Feathered Serpent", Quetzalcoatl, the most enduring of all Mesoamerican deities. Powerful shamanistic rituals and public ceremonies of blood-letting and human sacrifice became dominant themes in Mesoamerican civilization.

Around 400 BCE, La Venta was destroyed, its finest monument intentionally defaced. But the Olmec legacy of art, architecture, and ideology was a foundation for the elaborate cultural developments that followed. Their ideas of kingship, governance, and religious beliefs, spread rapidly. A century later, Mesoamerican societies changed rapidly as common ideologies united much of Central America for the first time. The leaders of the new religious orders understood the crucial importance of public spectacle and consolidated their influence with elaborate public ceremonies in spectacular architectural settings. Precise measurements of calendar years and longer time spans became essential. Written script and mathematics helped weld scattered village communities into much larger political units.

By the time the classic Mesoamerican civilizations of the lowlands and highlands arose, dynasties of lords had been ruling Mesoamerica along well-established lines for nearly a thousand years. The foundations of civilization were in place by two thousand years ago. But, despite many common beliefs and institutions, highland and lowland civilizations diverged in significant ways.

HIGHLANDS: THE VALLEY OF OAXACA (2000 TO 500 BCE)

The warm, semi-arid valley of Oaxaca, the homeland of the modern-day Zapotec people, is a highland plateau. Water lies close to the surface here, which allowed the local maize and bean farmers to plant their crops close to shallow wells. They then drew the water from the exposed water table with clay vessels and irrigated their crops. Thus, small numbers of people could irrigate and grow soils. As populations grew, so villagers expanded their agriculture onto more arid land and hillsides with great success.

Some of the valley's settlements grew to considerable size. The simple barter networks of earlier times developed into sophisticated regional trading associations controlled by village leaders that handled such commodities as obsidian and magnetite (used to make ritual mirrors), tropical bird feathers, and clay vessels. Oaxaca was in a strategic position to trade with both highlands and lowlands. Between 1150 and 650 BCE, Olmec pottery and other ritual objects appeared in the valley. Many of them bear the distinctive half-human, half-jaguar motif that was so important in Olmec ideology. By this time, many parts of both highland and lowland Mesoamerica shared common religious beliefs, even if there were numerous local deities and cults.

By 1300, a large village, San José Mogote, lay at the junction of three side valleys. Over the next century, it grew rapidly into a community of as many as 120 households living in rectangular houses with white-washed walls and thatched roofs. By this time, public buildings built on raised adobe and earth platforms, had appeared in larger Oaxacan settlements. Fish spines and conch trumpets, also other ritual objects, were symbols of more elaborate rituals. All of this occurred as a new Oaxacan elite aspired to the status of Olmec chiefs and mimicked their rituals and beliefs. The iconography of the jaguar and feathered serpent linked people of the highlands and lowlands alike.

In Oaxaca, at least seven small chiefdoms came under the influence of Monte Albán, founded on a hill overlooking the Valley. Soon, more than 5,000 people were living there, on a site that was far from the fertile soils at lower elevations. Perhaps its rulers chose the site as a symbol of power because it overlooked their domains. Between 350 and 200 BCE, over 16,000 people dwelt in the city, rising to a peak of 30,000 between 500 and 700 CE.

Monte Albán became an elaborate complex of palaces, temples, and plazas, the latter dedicated either to ritual practices or to markets. An enormous plaza, 300 meters long and 150 meters across, formed the core of the ceremonial precinct, which may have commemorated conquered kingdoms. Oaxaca's great city reached the height of its power after 200 BCE, when it rivaled another expanding state, Teotihuacán to the north. Monte Albán coexisted peacefully with its powerful rival. There was even a Oaxacan quarter there. But the center declined after about 750 CE, by which time its competitor was also losing power.

HIGHLANDS: TEOTIHUACÁN (C. 200 BCE TO 750 CE)

As early as 600 BCE, a series of chiefdoms presided over the valley of Mexico. When a volcanic eruption destroyed Cuicuilco, Teotihuacán's major rival, the surviving city grew dramatically. At least 80,000 people lived in Teotihuacán by 100 CE, growing to as many as 150,000 by 750. By that time it was as large as all but the largest cities in contemporary Southwest Asia or China.

This was no haphazard urban complex, but created according to a long-term masterplan, revealed by years of survey by the archaeologist René Millon among others. This was an enormous community, created by its architects not as a discrete city, but as a vast symbolic landscape of artificial mountains, foothills, caves, and open spaces that replicated the spiritual world. Over eight centuries, the Teotihuacános built 600 pyramids, 500 workshop spaces, a great market, 2,000 apartment complexes, and precinct plazas. All of this lay on a grid plan, anchored by the broad "Street of the Dead" (a modern name), which bisects the city on a north-south axis. Even today, deserted, partially restored, and devoid of its inhabitants, Teotihuacán overwhelms the visitor with its monumental size and scale. It dwarfs mere humans into insignificant dots as it was intended to do.

Between 1 and 100 CE, the colossal Pyramid of the Sun rose on the east side of the street. Sixty-one meters high with 215-meter sides, its five stages and immense stairway dwarf the nearby plaza and buildings. A tunnel dug into the original bedrock runs from the main stairway six meters below the surface into a clover-like set of four chambers that served as a cult center for some time after the pyramid was constructed. The smaller Pyramid of the Moon, built perhaps a century later, overlooks a plaza, surrounded by buildings at the north end of the street.

Three kilometers south, the broad street intersects with an east-west avenue that divides the city into four quarters. A huge enclosure at the intersection, known today as the Cuidadela ("citadel"), has sides over 400 meters long. Here lies the Temple of Quetzalcoatl, the Feathered Serpent. At least 200 sacrificial warriors went to their deaths with their hands tied behind their backs in groups of 18, the number of months in the Mesomerican year.

Teotihuacán was organized into wards based on kin ties and occupation. The elite dwelt in elaborate palaces with numerous rooms and forecourts. Commoners, soldiers, artisans, and traders lived in walled, residential compounds up to 60 meters long.

In its heyday, Teotihuacán covered at least 21 square kilometers. Artisans and traders from throughout the Mesoamerican world flocked there, attracted by commerce in green obsidian and all kinds of tropical products such as bird feathers. No one knows why the city's leaders expanded southward creating the Cuidadela by 225 CE. Perhaps it was during a period of successful conquests and great prosperity. The human sacrifices at the Temple of Quetzalcoatl may have been part of a cult of sacred war and human sacrifice that served to maintain the cosmos and human well-being. Thus, the Feathered Serpent's temple became the symbolic center of the universe.

For the next four centuries, the leadership may have become more collective and much more focused on ritual. To be a Teotihuacáno was to be honored, for one dwelt at the center of the world. Everyone served the state through artisanship, by labor on public works, or through service in the military. Teotihuacán's rulers controlled the destinies of about half a million people. Their power came from conquest and trade, and, above all, from a carefully nurtured ideology that made the city a place of creation, the cradle of civilization.

After about 650 CE, the great city floundered, partly because of rigid governance, perhaps drought, and also because of the enormous population that drained local resources. There may have been social disorder. The end came around a century later when Teotihuacán was apparently attacked and its temples, shrines, and palaces burned and reduced to rubble. Teotihuacán and its state dissolved, only to be remembered in legend, as a place of pilgrimage where later Toltec and Aztec civilizations came into being.

LOWLANDS: MAYA CIVILIZATION (C. 1200 BCE TO 1517 CE)

As the Olmec centers at San Lorenzo and La Venta achieved political influence, other centers with monumental architecture appeared in the Maya lowlands. Large platforms appeared at Ceibal in Guatemala's Petén as early as 1000 BCE. Ceibal shared many ritual practices as well as architecture with other emerging ceremonial centers. Some were of impressive size. At Aguada Fenix, in Mexico's Tabasco, a huge artificial platform covered 1,400 by 400 meters. The labor involved was colossal, but there are no signs of monumental statues or elaborate pyramids, as if systems of governance varied over the lowlands at the time.

By 800 to 600 BCE, local leaders at Nakbe in the Mirador Basin had organized large public works, which included pyramids up to 18 meters high. El Mirador, 13.6 kilometers away, achieved much greater importance by 350 BCE. Eventually, the city with its imposing buildings and pyramids atop low ridges surrounded by seasonally flooded swamps, covered 4 to 5 square kilometers. Like those at other Maya centers, the Mirador pyramids were built in many layers that can be peeled back by modern-day excavators. Their digs reveal parts of the original stucco façades with their enormous, brightly colored masks and friezes depicting deities and mythical scenes. Tens of thousands of people must have lived around the monumental center. Despite recent LiDAR surveys, accurate population estimates elude us.

A network of causeways linked El Mirador to smaller centers. What form of rulership was involved is uncertain, but a frieze in a buried Preclassic temple at San Bartolo, 58 kilometers southeast of El Mirador, contains a glyph that depicts *ayaw*, meaning "lord". The paintings in the frieze, a narrative of the Maya creation, have been radiocarbon-dated to between 400 and 200 BCE, the earliest known date for Maya kingship.

By 150 CE, El Mirador went into rapid decline and was soon depopulated. Quite why this and other Preclassic centers vanished remains a mystery. There are signs of warfare, always a reality in ancient Maya society. Drastic environmental changes also played a role, caused in part by climate change and deforestation by rising farming populations, and a rapidly growing demand for firewood to make lime plaster for facing pyramids.

CLASSIC MAYA CIVILIZATION (200 TO 900 CE)

The demise of well-established Preclassic centers coincided with centuries of prosperous Mesoamerican civilization. In the highlands, Monte Albán and Teotihuacán were entering their centuries of greatest power and influence, which extended into the lowlands. Maya civilization enjoyed a rebirth, too, as new cities emerged as major players. The changes coincided with major agricultural innovations, among them the increasing use of terracing and swamp agriculture. This was when Maya kingship came into its own, in the hands of rulers who bore the title "K'uhul Ajaw" (Holy Lord). This was the pivot on which entire city-states depended, presided over by powerful lords who used both their elaborate regalia and carefully staged, spectacular public ceremonies to emphasize their close relationships with mythical ancestral deities. New cities and new political organizations, came into play. Dynasties of rulers presiding over centers like Tikal, Calakmul, and Copán established their supernatural authority over lesser leaders and the populace as a whole. All of this revolved around the unfolding calendar, which regulated the unchanging routine of ceremonies and rituals that followed one another at major and minor centers.

Mayan hieroglyphic script came into being as a way of calculating calendars and thereby regulating religious observations. Its use was confined to rulers and the elite, with scribes assuming great importance. In times of war, their captors mutilated their fingers to prevent them writing. There was also a third, linear calendar of non-repeating linear days, which began on a mythical date, August 11, 3114 BCE, known today as the "Long Count." Above all, the calendar served an important role in kingship, for the royal crown passed from father to son, or brother to brother to son, back to a royal ancestor. One's ranking in the nobility depended on one's distance from the central royal descent line, so genealogy was of great importance.

Maya lords of the Classic period believed they had a divine covenant with the gods and the ancestors. They were the "world tree", the conduit by which humans communicated with the Otherworld. This worldview formed a lasting social contract between rulers and their nobles, and with commoners. The king acted as the state shaman, the organizer of trade and agriculture, and leader of part of a mosaic of political units large and small. The Maya world was volatile, a story of rising city-states like Tikal or Copán, which expanded their territory through diplomacy, political marriages, and conquest. Their domains grew early, then fractured as some of their provinces broke away and became independent, the state would then decline and dissolve into political insignificance.

There were four major Classic Maya city-states: Tikal, Palenque, Calakmul, and Copán. Tikal was a small farming village in 600 BCE, but soon developed into a much larger community. By the 2nd century CE, more than 40,000 people lived in or around the urban core (Figure 11.2). The founding ancestor was Yax-Ch'aktel-Xok (219–238 CE) ("First Scaffold Shark"), followed by a royal dynasty that lasted for 669 years of recorded history. During these centuries, an imposing central area included monumental structures, pyramids, and royal burial vaults centered around a large plaza surrounded by pyramids that were symbolic mountains. The stucco temple façades bore large masks, including some of rulers.

Figure 11.2 The central precincts of Tikal.

Tikal had regular trading contact with Teotihuacán in the high-lands and imported green obsidian, as well as acquiring militaristic philosophies of war and conquest. At the height of its power in the early 6th century, Tikal ruled over 2,500 square kilometers and 360,000 people, domains somewhat larger than Sumerian city-states in Mesopotamia 3000 years earlier. In about 557 CE, Tikal went into decline and was defeated by a rising state, Caracol, only to rise again in later centuries. The see-saw of rise and fall continued as Calakmul became a rival of Tikal between 514 and 814 CE, notable for its network of raised earth-packed or stone-packed roads that traversed swamps. Its ceremonial precinct covered about two square kilometers, with at least 50,000 people living in the surrounding residential area that spread over 20 square kilometers.

Copán, in present-day Honduras, boasted of an elaborate complex of courtyards, pyramids, and temples, an "Acropolis" that is an archaeological jigsaw. Over four centuries from 435 CE, the Blue Quetzal Macaw dynasty ruled the growing city, which became a major force in the Maya world. After a varied history, Copán was top-heavy with privilege-hungry nobles. By 771 CE, political unrest was widespread and Maya populations were declining rapidly. Most of the time local rulers looked after their own interests. Capable leaders who could unify several small kingdoms were rare.

Maya civilization reached its peak after 600 CE. Then, at the end of the 8th century, the great ceremonial centers of what is now Guatemala's Petén and the southern lowlands were abandoned. Tikal, perhaps the greatest Maya center, saw its population decline to a third of its earlier level. What is commonly known as the Classic Maya collapse has been the subject of debate for generations. Numerous factors came into play, some of them ecological, others social and political. Endemic warfare may have been one cause, for example, as witnessed at Dos Pilas in northern Guatemala.

Generations of warfare caused agricultural productivity to fall catastrophically. Population densities soared to as many as 200 people per square kilometer in places, making it impossible to clear new land. Long-term environmental degradation was a contributing factor. So were drought cycles, well documented in cave speleothems, rainfall declining as much as 36 to 52 percent below modern-day levels. There was no overriding cause of the collapse, but settlement studies around Copán document serious urban depopulation as the city's population moved into smaller villages. The ruling dynasty ended in 810 CE. Within three centuries, the city's population had fallen to as low as 5,000 people. Deforestation, over-exploitation of even marginal farming land, and uncontrolled erosion all played parts in the collapse at Copán and elsewhere.

The Classic Maya collapse was an episode, albeit an important one, in a long history of flowering, then collapse, in a society with an agricultural system that declined as a result of earlier over-exploitation. There were political and social developments as well, as the pattern of long-distance trade moved northward in the Yucatán, undercutting the ancient economies of earlier cities.

POSTCLASSIC MAYA CIVILIZATION (900 TO 1517 CE)

Despite the disintegration of city-states in the southern lowlands, Maya religious and social orders still endured in the more open country of the northern Yucatán. Northern centers like Uxmal and Chichen Itzá rose to prominence as coastal trade thrived. There was as much volatility in Postclassic Maya civilization as in earlier times. The Puuc Maya center of Uxmal near the modern city of Merida developed remarkable public architecture with imposing masonry buildings finished with veneers of well-cut stone. But first, the Puuc centers declined, followed by Chichen Itzá during the 13th century. Mayapan, near Merida, took advantage of the political vacuum and became a densely populated walled trading city of about 12,000 inhabitants ruling over a confederacy of smaller states. But the alliances fell apart during the mid-15th century.

Three quarters of a century later, in 1517, Spanish ships under the command of Francisco Hernández de Córdoba sailed along the densely populated coast, where they landed several times and collected golden ornaments. In 1519, Hernán Cortés landed on the Gulf Coast and headed inland, not in search of Maya treasure, but the gold-rich Aztec empire in the highlands.

HIGHLANDS: TOLTECS AND AZTECS (C. 900 TO 1521 CE)

The disintegration of Teotihuacán gave way to various small states that rose and fell in rapid order. Eventually, the Toltecs achieved a measure of dominance. Later Aztec propaganda elevated them to the level of great warrior heroes, who performed great deeds. In fact, they were an agglomeration of various tribal groups. According to Aztec accounts, they settled in the valley of Mexico, where a legendary ruler named Topiltzin Quetzalcoatl assumed the throne in 923 CE. It was he who was said to have founded a capital named Tollan, meaning "among the reeds" or more figuratively, and owing to its population density, "the place where people are thick as reeds", otherwise known to archaeologists as Tula.

By 1000 CE, Tula's rulers had laid out an imposing plaza surrounded by pyramids. This was a state of powerful warrior orders, much preoccupied with warfare and human sacrifice. The Toltec empire controlled much of Central Mexico during the 11th and 12th centuries, its prosperity based on trade and tribute. But it fell apart around 1200 CE, when Tula was razed, perhaps by Chichimeca people from outside the valley of Mexico who were pressing onto cultivated lands.

A small and obscure group, the Azteca or Mexica, stepped onto a political stage of competing minor kingdoms. Within a mere two centuries, these obscure players presided over the mightiest

Pre-Columbian empire in the Americas. Fierce and relentless war-riors, the Aztecs settled on swampy islands in the marshes of the great lake in the valley. There they founded twin capitals, Tenochti-tlán and Tlatelolco, sometime after 1325. By 1426, the Aztec were the masters of the valley of Mexico under an exceptionally able ruler, Itzcoatl, and his adviser Tlacaelel.

The two men invented a rags-to-riches history in a masterpiece of political propaganda. This held that they entered the valley of Mexico under the guidance of their tribal deity, Huitzilopochtli, "Hummingbird on the Left", soon to be reborn as the sun god. Their fabricated history made the Aztecs the chosen of Huitzilo-pochtli and the true heirs of the warrior Toltecs, destined to take prisoners of war to feed the sun god. A series of brilliant rulers now embarked on aggressive campaigns of conquest culminating in the campaigns of Ahuitzotl (1486–1502), the sixth Aztec ruler, or *tlatoani*, "speaker". He marched his armies far beyond the valley of Mexico, over wide tracts of the highlands and lowlands. Ahuit-zotl forged a flamboyant empire based on conquest and ruthlessly efficient tribute-gathering. His mission was to nourish his divine patron. Twenty thousand prisoners are said to have perished when he dedicated the rebuilt temple in the heart of Tenochtitlán in 1487, dedicated to Huitzilopochtli and the rain god Tlaloc, a site recently exposed by long-term excavations.

In 1519, Hernán Cortés and his conquistadors marveled at a city larger than Seville and better planned than many European capitals of the day. Thousands of hectares of carefully laid out swamp gardens intersected by canals fed the capital, with a population of between 200,000 and 400,000 inhabitants. The capital was the symbolic cen-ter of the Aztec universe, their mythical place of origin, Aztlan.

Despite the overarching ideology, the Aztec empire was far from a monolithic, highly centralized state. It was a mosaic of ever-chang-ing alliances, cemented together by an elaborate tribute-gathering machine. Everything was run for a growing elite, who maintained power by ruthless taxation, political marriage, and the constant threat of military force if tribute was not forthcoming. The state was run for the benefit of the rulers and nobility, who controlled land and exerted the right to use communal labor. Strictly enforced dress codes using capes enabled everyone to assess the rank of their wearers at a glance. The empire depended heavily on professional merchants, *pochteca*, who served as the eyes and ears of the state. The capital's great market at Tlatelolco was a mirror of a cosmopolitan empire. The Spanish conquistador Bernal Díaz recorded that at least 20,000 people a day attended the market, 50,000 on market days. An army of inspectors presided over commerce in everything from gold and silver to slaves, tropical bird feathers, capes, and firewood.

None of the Aztecs' political and social institutions were new, for Teotihuacán and the Toltecs had developed them. Ties of kin and a carefully administered system of neighborhoods, known as "calpulli" or big houses, served as a way of raising armies, and kept kin ties and family obligations at the center of daily life.

The Aztec empire was its height when Ahuitzotl died in 1501. A year later, Moctezuma Xocotyozin was elected in his place. Sixteen years afterwards, reports reached Moctezuma of white, bearded visitors to the Maya in the Yucatán. He and his advisers were at a loss to identify the newcomers. Meanwhile, Cortés decided to invade Aztec domains. To prevent desertion by his conquistadors, he burned his ships and advanced into the valley of Mexico at the head of an army of conquistadors and dissatisfied Aztec allies. In 1521, the greatest city in the Americas collapsed like a deck of cards and lay in smoking ruins. Ten years passed before the whole of Mexico (now New Spain) was under secure Spanish control. Ten of thousands of people perished, hundreds of thousands more from newly-introduced European diseases like influenza and smallpox. A rapid break-up of the Aztec state was inevitable in the face of overwhelming technological superiority. More than three thousand years of Mesoamerican civilization passed rapidly into centuries of historical obscurity.

★★★

The Temple of Huitzilopochtli, Tenochtitlán, 1487 CE... The shrine to the sun god stands high above the city, where the priests are about their work. A line of brightly clothed prisoners of war, adorned with feathers, climb up to meet their deaths. When the victim reaches the sacred precinct with its bloody altar, two priests stretch him out across the stone. A quick blow: a priest breaks open his chest with an obsidian knife, rips out the still-beating heart, then dashes it against the sacrificial stone. His assistants roll the bloody corpse down the pyramid into the hands of waiting butchers. They dismember the body and set its skull on the great skull rack nearby. Moments later, another victim goes to his death high above.

FURTHER READING

Susan Toby Evans, *Ancient Mexico and Central America*, 3rd ed. (London and New York: Thames & Hudson, 2013), is a definitive synthesis that covers Mesoamerican civilizations. Michael Coe and Rex Koontz, *Mexico: From the Olmecs to the Aztecs*, 6th ed. (London and New York: Thames and Hudson, 2008), covers much of the ground in this chapter. Christopher Poole, *Olmec Archaeology and Early Mesoamerica* (Cambridge: Cambridge University Press, 2007), Kent Flannery and Joyce Marcus, *Zapotec Civilizations* (London and New York: Thames & Hudson, 1996), and Kathleen Berrin and Esther Paztory (eds), *Teotihuacán: Art from the City of the Gods* (New York: Thames & Hudson, 1993), are invaluable publications. Michael Coe, *The Maya*, 8th ed. (London and New York: Thames & Hudson, 2011), is a classic. The Aztecs: Michael Smith, *The Aztecs,* 3rd ed. (Oxford: Blackwell, 2012), is an admirable general account.

ANDEAN CIVILIZATIONS (C. 3000 BCE TO 1532 CE)

Chavín de Huantar, Andes foothills, Peru, 800 BCE... Steady rain and wood smoke mingle with cascading incense above the plazas and temples of the ancient shrine. Hidden passages inside the Old Temple thunder with fast-flowing water. The watching crowd watches in silence, oblivious to the damp. A conch trumpet sounds. Suddenly, a masked shaman appears in a hallucinogenic trance. He chants and sings, utters the pronouncements from the oracle. Then he vanishes into the depths of the shrine with its maze of hidden passages. Hidden, sacred conch shell trumpets sound. The droning sound in the unseen chambers embraces the crowd in the plaza. As the pitch changes, the sound seems to come from several places, adding to the sense of confusion, awe, and supernatural fear.

The much later Inca called their domains Tawantinsuyu, "the Land of the Four Parts". In the 15th century CE, their empire extended along the Andes mountains and across the *altiplano*, the high plains of the Lake Titicaca basin. The Pacific was the western boundary; Amazon forests lapped its eastern edge. Both the highlands and the Pacific lowlands contributed to the fabric of the civilizations that developed centuries before the Inca mastered some of the most diverse landscapes on earth.

Over many centuries, two poles of Andean civilization developed—one in the south-central highland Andes, the other along the north

DOI: 10.4324/9781003177326-12

Figure 12.1 Sites mentioned in Chapter 12.

coast of what is now Peru. The southern pole comprises the altiplano and the Lake Titicaca basin, also highland Bolivia and adjacent areas. The northern end of the Titicaca Basin is somewhat warmer and better watered, which makes it possible to herd both alpacas and llamas, and to cultivate quinoa, also potatoes. This was where the powerful Tiwanaku state flourished during the first millennium CE.

The northern pole lay along the arid and, essentially rainless, Peruvian coastal plain, which extends south nearly 550 kilometers (Figure 12.1). The widest portion extends inland about 100 kilometers around the Lambayeque Valley. About forty rivers bring mountain runoff to the coast, but only a few low-lying desert areas could be used for irrigation. The most densely settled areas where irrigation was possible lay in the Chicama/Moche and Lambayeque areas. Here, farmers could use canals to bring water to their fields from several rivers, supporting denser populations. Fortunately, natural upwelling from the sea bed close offshore provided rich anchovy fisheries so predictable that sedentary base camps flourished for generations along the coast. This was an arid landscape, with only the unpredictable El Niños weather system bringing significant rainfall.

PRECERAMIC SOCIETIES (C. 3000 TO 1800/1200 BCE)

After about 5,000 BCE, fishing became more important along the Pacific, so much so that some communities moved into larger, relatively sedentary communities. At Paloma on the Chica River on the central coast, the inhabitants relied heavily on fishing. They netted thousands of anchovies close inshore, but also caught deep water fish, using spears from canoes. Edible plants were also an important part of the diet at this village only 4.5 kilometers from the ocean. There was also some deliberate manipulation of edible plant foods.

The domestication of plants and animals took hold by 3000 BCE. Alpacas and llamas were domesticated by 2500 BCE, the latter becoming valuable pack animals capable of carrying 16-kilogram loads. At least four species of tubers became staples—oca, mashua, and ullucu, this apart from the potato, first domesticated in the Lake Titicaca region. The staple cereal crops were maize and quinoa, the former, first domesticated in Mesoamerica, may have been an important coastal staple as early as 3000 BCE.

By 3000 BCE, coastal society was much more complex. One coastal compound at Aspero boasted of platform mounds and covered at least 15 hectares in about 3055 BCE. Caral, 22.5 kilometers from the Pacific and 193 kilometers north of Peru's current capital of Lima, was a large town as early as 3000 BCE. The 81-hectare settlement surrounded a central zone with six platform mounds built of quarried stone and river cobbles, arranged around a large plaza. The highest is 18 meters high and measured 137 by 152 meters at its base. All the mounds were built in one or two phases, almost certainly at the behest of a powerful centralized authority capable of organizing large labor forces, who carried netfuls of rocks to the site.

Caral was one of as many as seventeen centers in the Supe valley region supported by irrigation agriculture. The crops included both maize and potatoes, also cotton. Here, as elsewhere along the coast, anchovies were a major part of the diet. We know almost nothing about the leaders who constructed Caral, who somehow commanded the loyalty of the hundreds, if not thousands, of commoners who built their imposing centers. Caral was the largest settlement in the Americas in its day, rising just as the pharaohs built pyramids in Egypt. Nor do we know why the site was abandoned between 1500 and 2000 BCE, just as other kingdoms came to power along the north coast.

Why did states arise along this arid coastline? Clearly, anchovies and other marine resources helped support growing coastal populations. Most likely, a combination of irrigation agriculture and fishing contributed to the dramatic changes in coastal societies. These food sources provided the surpluses that support the building of increasingly large ceremonial centers.

Both in the lowlands and highlands, states came about in part because of continuous exchanges between groups on the coast, in the mountain foothills, and on the highlands. Farmers at higher elevations needed salt, also protein-rich fish meal, and seaweed, which is rich in iodine and useful for combating a variety of medical conditions. The highlands contributed carbohydrate-rich foods like oca, white potatoes, which could not be grown at low elevations, and ulluco. A combination of vigorous trade, maritime foods and intensive irrigation, the cultivation of beans, cotton, and maize in coastal river valleys controlled by well-defined authority figures, led to major changes in Andean society.

HIGHLANDS AND LOWLANDS: TOWARDS CIVILIZATION (C. 2000 TO 500 BCE)

By 2000 BCE, some coastal villages became large communities, with highly organized social institutions. Their leaders were now able to build large ceremonial sites. El Paraiso in the Chillon valley in the central coast near Lima was remarkable for its U-shaped platform, the open end facing upstream. Pyramids formed the base of the U both here and elsewhere. Surrounding mounds enclosed the courtyard within its several sunken courts, like those built at Caral as early as 2600 BCE. Such courts made sure that visitors entered the sacred complex at ground level, then climbed to the summit of the temple platform. El Paraiso was built of more than 100,000 tons of local rock, apparently with labor provided by surrounding villages. The ceremonial center had few residential inhabitants, but was a place where people from a wider area gathered for major public ceremonies.

Similar U-shaped platforms now adorned ceremonial centers along the north coast, decorated with elaborate adobe friezes and powerful visual imagery. A forty-meter high platform is almost 300 meters long and forms the base of a stone-faced, U-shaped ceremonial precinct at Sechín Alto in the Casma Valley. A nearby site lies atop a low hill and contains almost 400 engraved slabs that show a procession of armed men with clubs or staffs passing among maimed human victims, and their mutilated body parts. The monoliths display vivid mythic and religious scenes that commemorate warfare and human sacrifice.

Between 1000 and 800 BCE, a series of small kingdoms developed along the north and central coast. These kingdoms traded continuously with one another and with those in the highlands. Many ceremonial centers came into being, but leadership seems to have been based on kin ties. Irrigation agriculture intensified in coastal locations where ample labor forces were at hand, slopes were gentle, and soils were fertile when watered. Initially, irrigation was probably organized by family groups, but the community became so large that essential farming works could only be handled cooperatively, which led to ancestors of the *mit'a* labor tax system of later centuries. People worked a certain number of days a year for the state either as construction workers, or farmers. They were paid in food, shelter, and sometimes received a share of crops from state lands. Eventually, elaborate public works involved entire valleys, controlled by a central authority that monopolized water supplies and the irrigated land.

HIGHLANDS: CHAVÍN DE HUANTAR (C. 1500–500 BCE)

Many material, social, and spiritual threads created Andean civilization, But few were as influential as the beliefs from Chavín de Huantar, which lies in a small valley 3,000 meters above sea level midway between the Pacific and the tropical rainforest east of the mountains. This was a strategic location for trade routes between the lowlands and highlands. Between 1250 and 500 BCE, the trading center became an important place of pilgrimage.

Between 2,000 and 4,000 BCE people lived beside the river near to an imposing temple in the heart of the community. Construction at the site peaked between 1000 and 800 BCE, with the building of a constantly modified temple with underground passages and distinctive artwork. The U-shaped temple design of earlier times became part of the temple, the central court open to the east towards sunrise, and the rainforest. It was a maze of small rooms, passages, and galleries, ventilated by special rectangular tubes. A white granite monolith built into the floor and ceiling, known as the *Lanzon,* "lance", stands in a cross-shaped chamber near the central axes of the oldest part of the temple.

What rituals took place here? Chavín art features dramatic representations of animals and humans. Jaguar motifs predominate, while gods, humans, and other animals have jaguar-like fangs or limbs. Snakes flow from the bodies of many figures. There were two gods at Chavín. The Lanzon has a human body and feline face, hands, and feet. The "Staff" god was a standing male with downturned, snarling face, and serpent headdress. He grasps two staffs, each adorned with feline heads and jaguar mouths. The Lanzon and the Staff god were anthropomorphic deities, probably symbols of ritual transformations between the living and the spiritual that were enacted in the Old Temple. A granite slab from the temple plaza shows a jaguar-human in full regalia grasping a hallucinogenic San Pedro cactus, still used by local shamans today. The mescaline in the cactus has mind-altering effects that bestow impressive powers. Animals, humans, and plants were always interconnected in the flamboyant Chavín ideology. The beliefs were so compelling, born as they were of forest, mountain, and desert, that they influenced entire human societies and art styles over an enormous area. Chavín was one of the great catalysts for Andean civilization, for its ideologies spread widely on painted textile wall hangings, and on artifacts in clay, gold, and wood.

SOUTHERN HIGHLANDS: TIWANAKU (C. 100 TO 1000 CE)

As Chavín rose to prominence in the northern highlands, a separate cultural tradition developed around Lake Titicaca far to the south. Between 1400 and 100 BCE, Chiripa in the southern shore of the lake added farming and herding to its traditional fishing and fowling. It remained a small village until about 1000 BCE, when the first platform mound appeared in the community. Over the centuries, the platform was enlarged until it was 6 meters high; it also featured a sunken court.

Chiripa flourished as autonomous, permanent villages developed in prime areas near lakes and rivers in the Titicaca basin. Some of them became regional political centers. At first things were apparently peaceful, but artworks depict such telltale sign of warfare as trophy heads after 500 BCE. By two thousand years ago, several larger regional centers had developed in an intensely competitive political, militant landscape. By 200 CE, Tiwanaku at the southern end of Titicaca was a major population center. Its leaders developed widespread trade connections, carried by llama caravans that linked the highlands and the southern coast.

Tiwanaku became a major economic and religious force within three centuries. The growing center prospered from copper technology (developed independently from the lowlands), and fine textiles that traveled by caravan as far as the coast. During and after the 8th century, Tiwanaku controlled elaborate, irrigated, raised field systems that covered at least 75 square kilometers. These supported at least 20,000 people, with many more in the surrounding valleys. Modern experiments have shown that raised fields are frost resistant and highly productive in potato crops, with yields as much as 400 percent higher than those from drier plots on surrounding hillsides.

Meanwhile, Tiwanaku assumed enormous ritual importance. The great enclosure and temple of Kalasasaya includes a large earth platform faced with stones, and aligned with the cardinal points of the compass. An arch carved with an anthropomorphic deity, believed to be the creator god Viracocha, stands adjacent. The nearby Akapana, an artificial platform with a sunken continent at the summit, about 200 meters long and 15 meters high, dominates the city. During the rains, water would gush out of the court onto the terraces, flowing into a large moat that surrounded the ceremonial precincts.

Archaeologist Alan Kolata, who has spent years studying Tiwanaku, believes the precincts served as a symbolic island, like the sacred island of the sun in nearby Lake Titicaca. This was where Tiwanaku's leaders would appear, dressed like gods in full regalia and elaborate headdresses. Theirs was a powerful iconography marked by human sacrifice that prevailed over an empire held together by tightly controlled trade, carefully planned conquest, and deliberate colonization.

Tiwanaku's empire survived longer than other Andean states of the day, but appears to have succumbed to a major drought cycle during the 11th century. The central government collapsed, field systems fell into disrepair, and the empire disintegrated.

NORTH COAST: MOCHE CIVILIZATION (C. 1–700 CE)

A new political and social order came into being on the coast about 2,000 years ago. Changes in architectural styles marked the change, especially the construction of *huacas* (monuments) on a large scale. These were often steep, mudbrick pyramids. By 100 CE, the Moche state, a new and powerful form of Andean civilization, had emerged from earlier roots. This was never a completely unified entity, but a patchwork of smaller groups centered on river valleys large and small, each ruled by local elites. The Moche homeland revolved round larger valleys in the north, such as the Lambayeque.

Economic and political power derived from military conquest, an ability to impose control over weaker neighbors and defense against outsiders. Complex alliances, political marriages, and other deal-ings linked ruling elites in different centers. Above all, a powerful and rigidly imposed ideology held the state together. Having no Moche script, we know of it indirectly from its decorative iconogra-phy, magnificent ritual objects, and formal regalia discovered in elite burials. The settings for celebrating this ideology were spectacular temples.

Cerro Blanco in the Moche Valley was the most spectacular cen-ter. Two enormous adobe structures, Huaca del Sol (monument/ pyramid of the sun) and Huaca de la Luna (monument/pyramid of the moon) rose close to one another. Huaca del Sol was more than 40 meters high, a royal palace and burial ground, the façade painted in red and other colors. Huaca de la Luna had three platforms con-nected by low adobe walls adorned with brightly colored murals of mythic anthropomorphic and zoomorphic figures. In a secluded part of the temple, 70 warriors were sacrificed, then dismembered. At least two of these sacrificial rituals occurred when heavy El Niño rains descended on the Moche Valley. Michael Moseley believes that the two huacas reflect powerful, centralized rule, the temple built in segments by teams of *mit'a* (mandatory public service laborers) over many generations. This labor tax was essential to build and maintain increasingly elaborate irrigation systems. Much of the cultivated land lying on the terraced sides of valleys, was fed by irrigation canals winding alongside.

The Moche elites were at the height of their power around 500 CE, coopting conquered rulers and their domains into political systems that were also used by the late Chimú and Inca. But a series of powerful El Niños, also political and military unrest, as well as unsuccessful adaptions to local conditions, brought chaos to the Moche homeland. The state dissolved into a closely knit mosaic of smaller kingdoms in about 700 CE.

Who ruled the Moche? They were of diverse origin, with intricate kin relationships, and economic ties. Their wealth and artistic sophistication was remarkable. In 1987, tomb robbers targeted an apparently unprepossessing pyramid at Sipán in the Lambayeque Valley. Subsequent archaeological investigations have revealed over 14 royal burials, awash in gold, silver, and copper. Each Moche lord wore his full ceremonial regalia with elaborate tunics, fine headdresses and back flaps, also golden face ornaments and carried such ceremonial rattles, exotic seashells, and fine weapons. Sacrificial victims accompanied them. Moche expert Christopher Donnan believes they were "warrior-priests" at the pinnacle of Moche society, men with immense political and spiritual power. They presided over ritual sacrifices of war prisoners and drank their blood (Figure 12.2).

What we know of the Moche comes from burials, studies of (often looted) pots, and artwork. Artists and artisans depicted Moche warriors charging their opponents with raised clubs and fighting to the death. There are sculpted, realistic portraits of elite men with arrogant, calm expressions, of befuddled drunks, even of sex acts and childbirth. We see a llama straining under a heavy load, men clubbing seals, and a mouse eating a maize cob.

Rigidly governed Moche society came apart over several centuries, but the collapse of political authority may have resulted from the failure of long-established strategies that used ideology to maintain power. As ideology loosened, so society changed and the Moche elite vanished into history.

Figure 12.2 The burial of a Moche Lord of Sipán in full regalia.

Wening/Alamy Stock Photo

THE COAST: SICÁN AND CHIMOR (C. 1100–1400 CE)

After 700 CE, the Sicán kingdom, centered on the Lambayeque Valley, achieved significant wealth, marked by metal ornaments that denoted prestige, and social and religious standing. Sicán lords developed massive irrigation works as well as metallurgy. Oral traditions hint that the lords from various centers, often linked by irrigation canals, shared common ancestors. Their wealth was fabulous. One forty- to fifty-year-old man was interred, upside down, in a roofed burial chamber in full regalia, including an elaborate golden mask and gloves. But between 1050 and 1100 CE, a massive El Niño event caused widespread flooding and disruption, as political power shifted southward. In 1375 CE, the expanding Chimú empire (Chimor) absorbed Sicán into its domains.

Chimor was born of the political uncertainty that followed the demise of the Moche state. During the 13th century, Chimor's leaders embarked on a vigorous campaign of conquest and expansion, which continued on and off for two centuries. They soon absorbed Sicán and the Lambayeque Valley. By 1470 CE, Chimor controlled over 1,000 kilometers of the coastline and an area that included no less than two-thirds of all the irrigated land along the Peruvian coast. For the first time, a single state ruled the northern pole of Andean civilization.

Chimú's rulers embarked on ambitious irrigation projects. They constructed large storage reservoirs and terraced thousands of kilometers of hillsides to control the flow of water down steep slopes. The secrets of their success lay both in tight, centralized administration and in their ability to move water over long distances. One channel extended nearly 20 kilometers from the Chicama Valley to the new capital, Chan Chan, in order supplement local water supplies. Their irrigation methods were so effective that they controlled more than twelve river valleys with at least 50,600 cultivable hectares, all farmed with simple technology—hoes and digging sticks. Judging from modern practice in the region, farmers watered their crops every ten days.

As the focus of this remarkable state was Chan Chan, a huge complex of walled compounds which covers nearly 20 square kilometers near the mouth of the Moche Valley. Nine large enclosures dominated the central precincts in a broken rectangle that covers about six square kilometers. Each was constructed by statuary *mit'a* labor as the palace and headquarters for the current ruler, who built his base near those of his predecessors. The enclosure walls gave privacy, and shelter from the ocean winds. Each had its own water supply, with lavishly decorated residential rooms, roofed with cane frames covered with earth and grass. When a ruler died, he lay under a burial platform in his enclosure, once reserved for deities. Some 6,000 nobles lived in smaller compounds with low walls, while 26,000 artisans and their families, many of them metalworkers and weavers, dwelt on the western side of the city center. Numerous farmers and fisherfolk dwelt further outside.

According to Chimú oral traditions, passed down verbally through the generations, between nine and eleven rulers governed from Chan Chan, each of them considered a god-king. They ruled through a network of hereditary nobility, who possessed grandiose titles. They included "The Preparer of the Way", an official who scattered powdered shell dust wherever the ruler was to walk. The elite enjoyed not only tribute privileges, but also rights to crops, land, and agricultural labor by commoners. This was a profoundly stratified society with a well-regulated social hierarchy.

Chimor's administration depended on efficient communications enhanced by the development of a road network. While much of it was little more than tracks, densely populated valleys had wide highways. These carried gold, textiles, and other commodities such as fine, black-painted vessels throughout the empire. Everything traveled on human backs or on those of llamas, the latter often traveling in caravans. Tributes and other revenues also passed along the highway as did people traveling in large numbers for compulsory resettlement in conquered lands, where they were governed by a noble loyal to the ruler. The policy of resettlement was so successful that the Inca adopted it.

The empire may have extended as far south as modern-day Lima, but its main center was the northern coast with its major potential for irrigation. With its wealth and wide-ranging military activity, Chimor was vulnerable to outside attack, and also to prolonged drought cycles. Between 1462 and 1470 CE, the ambitious leader Minchancamon fought constantly with the Inca. Eventually, the Inca prevailed and Chimor became part of Tawantinsuyu. Thousands of Chimú artisans were resettled in the Inca capital, Cuzco, to serve their new masters.

THE INCA EMPIRE (1476–1534 CE)

The collapse of Tiwanaku, and of its neighboring highland kingdom, Wari, left a political vacuum in the southern highlands. Many small kingdoms competed for power and trade monopolies. At the time, the Incas were a small-scale farming society of small villages organized in *ayllu*, ancient Andean kin groups. Later, Inca rulers boasted of epic deeds, but unreliable genealogies talk of at least eight, probably legendary leaders between 1200 and 1438 CE. By the early 15th century, Inca chiefs had turned from raiding neighboring kingdoms to serious conquest. They soon presided over a small kingdom based on their capital, Cuzco, where they embraced the cult of Inti, a celestial divine ancestor associated with the sun. Now they proclaimed themselves living gods.

A brilliant warrior, Cusi Inca Yupanqui, became ruler in 1438, assuming the name Pachakuti, "He Who Remakes the World." And remake it he did. Pachakuti reworked an ancient ancestor cult into a law of split inheritance. A dead ruler was mummified. His palace, servants, and possessions continued to serve him as a living god. Meanwhile, his successor, usually one of his sons, had to acquire wealth on his own account—and wealth in Inca society was taxable labor. The newcomer had to develop his own tax base, which meant that he had to conquer new territory to be controlled and taxed. Successive Inca leaders preached that the welfare of everyone depended on the prosperity of all rulers, past and present, and on military conquest. A highly complicated set of benefits, economic incentives, and rewards fueled and nourished Inca conquests. Within a decade of Pachakuti's accession, they were masters of the southern highlands. In less than a century, Pachakuti's tiny kingdom had become a vast empire. At its maximum extent, the diverse empire extended into Ecuador far to the north, with no less than eighty provinces under at least nominal Inca control.

An efficient administration system was essential for such an enormous and diverse empire. Tawantinsuyu was divided into four quarters (*suyu*), each subdivided into smaller provinces, all the important government posts being held by Inca nobles. Everything depended on fast, reliable communication, based on a vast network of ancient highways built by the people they had conquered. The system was coordinated with spaced-out rest houses, enabling the rapid deployment of armies, messengers, and trade goods from one end of the empire to the other.

This was just the beginning, for the Inca's passion for organization affected everyone. There were twelve age divisions for census purposes and tax assessment. The most important stage was adulthood, identified by the length of time it took a person to complete a day's work. Everything in Inca life stressed conformity and the need to respect and obey the central government.

As with any empire, an accurate census was essential. Like other Andean societies, the Inca did not develop written script. All census and other imperial data resided on *quipu*, a complex hierarchy of knotted cords in varying colors that enabled scribes to compile remarkably accurate inventories of animals, crop yields, land ownership, people, and so on. Unfortunately, the *quipu* code was lost with the arrival of the Spaniards, but it served as a powerful instrument of social control in the hands of traveling inspectors.

Inca political and religious power centered on Cuzco. Laid out on a cruciform plan, the city had enough water to allow open channels to flow through the streets. A wall of closely fitted masonry blocks surrounded the central precincts. The leaders' palaces and the *Qurikancha*, the Temple of the Sun or the "Sun House", lay inside, the latter built around a garden of golden plants and maize with silver stems and golden ears. Like most pre-industrial capitals, Cuzco was not only a capital, but an enormous repository. Rows of stone field houses contained vast inventories of ceremonial cloaks, metal objects, tropical bird feathers, weapons and tribute from all corners of Tawantinsuyu.

The supreme Inca held court in Cuzco, surrounded by plotting factions. The intrigue and stress heightened as the empire became larger and larger, thanks to the institution of split inheritance, which demanded unceasing conquest. The logistics of long-distance campaigning were horrendous. The administrative problems confronting the supreme ruler mounted amidst increasingly rebellious factions, many of them headed by nobles loyal to deceased rulers.

The façade was glittering, but the core was rotten.

When the Spanish conquistador Francisco Pizarro landed in Peru in 1531, Tawantinsuyu was in political chaos and descending into civil war. Smallpox and other diseases introduced by earlier European visitors to Central America were rife among the population. In 1533, Pizarro captured Cuzco with a tiny army. Three years later, a desperate rebellion by the then ruler Manco Inca resulted in the dismemberment of Tawantinsuyu, but not of its people, who thrive to this day.

★★★

Lambayeque Valley, northern Peru, c. 600 CE... The prisoners of war huddle together, coated with dust and dried blood. They are carefully guarded after dark, but are quiet, for they are all too aware of their fate. At dawn, the guards herd them down to the nearby river to wash. A large crowd has gathered by the temple plaza as drums beat and people dance in the morning sun. A conch trumpet sounds and the crowd grows silent. The ruler appears from the temple atop the pyramid in full regalia. His gold and silver ornaments commemorate the sun and moon. He sits as incense swirls, motionless, as a line of naked captives passes. Occasionally a noble prisoner joins the doomed procession, carried in a litter by his own men. Executioners cut the prisoners' throats before the brightly caparisoned lord. Then he drinks fresh blood from a ceremonial vessel, as do the priests and their attendants.

FURTHER READING

Michael Moseley, *The Inca and Their Ancestors*, 2nd ed. (London and New York: Thames & Hudson, 2000), is a definitive summary of Andean archaeology. Jerry Moore, *A Prehistory of South America* (Boulder, CO: University Press of Colorado, 2014), and William Isbell, *Andean Archaeology* (New York: Kluwer/Plenum), are also valuable. Chavín: Richard Berger, *Chavín and the Origins of Andean Civilization* (New York: Thames & Hudson, 1992). Jeffrey Quilter, *The Ancient Central Andes* (Abingdon: Routledge, 2013), is a useful general account. Walter Alva and Christopher Donnan, *Moche Lords of Sipán* (Los Angeles: Fowler Museum of Cultural History, 1993), is a magnificent account for the general reader. The Inca: Terence N. D'Altroy, *The Incas* (Oxford: Blackwell, 2002), is a good introduction.

EPILOGUE

We ended our journey through human prehistory high in the Andes. And what a journey, which began about 6 million years ago, continued into very recent times. But why should we study a human past that is sometimes unimaginably remote from today's industrialized world? Is it of any value when there is a global climatic crisis, widespread poverty, and a growing gap between rich and poor? Why should we spend precious resources investigating long vanished societies?

Today, the long-established stereotypes of eccentric professors in sun helmets digging in the shadow of pyramids, or of a swashbuckling Indiana Jones, are the stuff of fiction, nothing more. Archaeologists and their work have a pressing relevance in today's world. Let's not forget that the astrophysicist Carl Sagan reminded us that "You have to know the past to understand the present." To which we would add the future. Furthermore, today's highly sophisticated archaeology helps produce informed people capable of making rational decisions about such important issues as climate change, human diversity and equality, also governance, and sustainability.

In recent years, an increasing number of people, from politicians to educationalists, regard the past as a "foreign country," irrelevant in today's challenging world. This is nonsense. The past allows us to examine ourselves on a global scale, and with a long-term

DOI: 10.4324/9781003177326-13

perspective, of tens of thousands of years of human experience. As a result, we can question modern behavior—particularly when justifications for attitudes on specific issues such as racial differences are wrapped in outdated ideologies or, incredible though it may seem, outrageous conspiracy theories.

As our journey through prehistory has shown, much human experience is embedded in cultural continuity and change. And archaeology is the only science that allows us to explore these most fundamental questions over immensely long periods of time. In these pages, we've thought not in single years, but in millennia and centuries. Historians, who work primarily with written and documentary sources, tend to focus on much shorter periods, even days, hours, or minutes. Their research carries us back some 5000 years in Egypt and Mesopotamia. But before 3100 BCE, the landscape of ancient times extends far back into the distant past, explored by today's increasingly hi-tech archaeology.

The story in these pages results from thousands of excavations, surveys, and laboratory studies. It is a global story assembled laboriously over more than a century of increasingly fine-grained research. Today, we have at least a general idea of what happened in most parts of the world. We have a growing knowledge of human origins and of the spread of both archaic and modern humans through the world. We know that the first human settlement of the Americas unfolded after 15,000 years ago. Agriculture and animal husbandry came about in more than one place after 10,000 BCE. The earliest pre-industrial civilizations developed along the Nile and in Mesopotamia by 3100 BCE. Thereafter, state-organized societies, mostly with strongly centralized social organization, emerged in Africa, the Middle East, and Asia, also in the Americas. All of them shared some common features, among them marked social inequality, increasing cultural complexity, and a heavy dependence on food surpluses created by commoners to support large numbers of non-farmers.

Pre-industrial civilizations depended on animal power and human labor for wealth and prosperity. Many still-familiar practices and human institutions came into being with the appearance of urbanized states—despotic rule, the majority working for the benefit of a small elite, ardent militarism and a conviction that standing armies and force were appropriate mechanisms of governance—to mention but a few. If there is one common feature of all pre-industrial societies, it is that of volatility and an inability to control and maintain authority, over anything more than a relatively small core territory. There were exceptions, of course, most famous being that of Dynastic Egypt, which survived, albeit with hiccups, for 3000 years.

The emergence of world prehistory as a serious field of research is one of the great scientific achievements of the 20th century. But what comes next? And what does this laboriously acquired knowledge contribute to our understanding of ourselves—humanity?

In recent years, archaeology has changed radically. We used to focus on what happened and when—what is often called culture history. During the 1960s, we began to pay closer attention to explanation. Why, for example, did people turn to agriculture or found cities? But the greatest change came in the way we went about our business as archaeologists. Archaeologists have been cooperating with scientists since World War II and even earlier, but the embrace is now so close that we describe ourselves as multidisciplinary researchers. We work with radiocarbon dating methods that allow us to date a single seed, and to establish how many generations used a communal term. Isotopic studies of human teeth tell us where people lived in their youth. Sometimes we know more about their health than they did. LiDAR and other remote sensing methods strip away dense rainforest from Maya centers and Khmer temples in Southeast Africa, revealing entire ancient landscapes.

Our field and laboratory work is increasingly fine-grained, so much so that the focus of archaeological research has shifted from finding out what happened toward exploring issues that are of pressing importance in today's world. A new generation of research is adding fresh, and sometimes surprising, perspectives to the narrative of prehistory. Here are some of the new directions engaging us.

ANCIENT CLIMATE CHANGE

Human activities have been the dominant cause of global warming and climate change since the mid-20th century. Future climatic shifts monopolize the headlines, but the past provides a sobering background to today's debates. A revolution in paleoclimatology has highlighted dramatic, long- and short-term temperature and rainfall changes during the Ice Age and since then. Rich archives of climatic proxies like glacial cores, speleothems, and tree-rings, indirect records of ancient shifts, have transformed our knowledge of how humans have adapted to ever-changing climatic conditions. Since the Ice Age ended about 15,000 years ago, the changes have been relatively brief in the main, such as El Niño events and both long- and short-term drought cycles. There have, of course, been longer-term shifts as well, notably in retreats of ice sheets, rising sea levels, and major vegetational transformations.

Today, we think about climate change globally, whereas, in the past, much adaptation was purely local. Farmers confronted with longer-term droughts shifted to the cultivation of drought resistant crops; cattle farmers dispersed their herds, as they do in the Saharan Sahel today. Many societies had the luxury of mobility. People moved to areas with more predictable rainfall or reliable water supplies. Of course we cannot use ancient climate change to predict the future, especially since we live in a heavily urbanized world, where people cannot move. All of humanity is now in the same climatic boat. In the past, both simple and more complex societies were able to adapt, thanks to ties of kin and the ability of city dwellers to maintain ties with their rural roots. Human prehistory is a chronicle of ingenious human adaptations to climate change. It also reminds us that the solution to today's climatic challenges lies in long-term planning to make the world better for our descendants. Fortunately, our perspective on deeper history shows that when we humans are really up against things, we do take action, which should give us hope for the future.

HUMAN DIVERSITY

World prehistory embraces the history of every human on earth and celebrates the astounding diversity of our species. As archaeologists, we face formidable obstacles in analyzing our ancestry: ethnocentrism, racism, and outmoded colonial attitudes are among them. Many of these convictions stem from long discredited assumptions that humans, and societies, evolved from the simple to the complex in an orderly, linear fashion. As the great 19th-century biologists Charles Darwin and Thomas Huxley showed us, human biological and cultural diversity were far more complex. Now we have the tools to study this complexity. The sequencing of the human genome and the development of the "molecular clock" are allowing us to study evolutionary relationships over long timescales. Genetics is now playing a major role in the story told in these pages.

Human ancestry and diversity are one thing, but there is more. Archaeology can tell us a great deal about who we are because it provides identity to silenced groups, often called "the people without history". We study the non-literate societies omitted from conventional history books, also those who are sometimes called "the hidden"—commoners, slaves, women, ethnic minorities and others, who lived out their lives in the shadows of history. Generations of historians have studied kings, generals, and charismatic statesmen. Such people are, of course, part of the meat and drink of studying the human past. But the narrative of world prehistory has the potential to delve much more deeply into the diversity of ancient societies. For years, archaeologists have talked about restoring historical identities to entire societies, like, for example, African groups who first came into contact with literate societies in Victorian times.

ETHNOARCHAEOLOGY

Prehistory may have ended in Egypt and Mesopotamia in 3100 BCE, but traditional non-literate societies thrived in parts of tropical Africa until the late 19th century and in New Guinea and the Amazon rainforest into modern times. Ethnoarchaeology is the field study of traditional societies that have survived the trauma of the European Age of Discovery and the forces of colonialism. It is all very well to compare modern-day Inuit societies with late Ice Age hunter-gatherers, but much more valuable insights come from present-day research. For example, anthropologist Richard Lee's studies of San hunter-gatherers in southern Africa's Kalahari Desert have provided new insights into our perceptions of hunting and foraging societies as have the lengthy studies of Amazonian societies and people living in the New Guinea highlands; likewise the inestimable agricultural expertise of Pueblo farmers of the American Southwest is at risk of disappearance. Yet only now are we beginning to understand the full legacy of our forebears, not only from anthropological fieldwork, but also from efforts to recover the unwritten history of millions of people living at the subsistence level, whose histories can only be recovered from oral traditions and archaeology.

BIOARCHAEOLOGY

Apart from genetics, the powerful weaponry of today's medical researchers has enabled us to study people of the past. We know all about the health problems of the Egyptian pharaoh Rameses II and now, using medical X-ray scanning, we have facial reconstructions of Tutankhamun and other well-known figures from ancient times. But we can do much more. In 2470 BCE, a man aged between 35 to 45 years old was buried at Amesbury, about 5 kilometers southeast from Stonehenge in the south of England. He was an archer, buried with his bow. He suffered from an abscess in his jaw, had lost his left kneecap in an accident, and he walked with a straight foot that swung out to his left. A bone infection caused him constant pain. But he had been a serious traveler. An oxygen isotope analysis of his teeth revealed that he had grown up in the Swiss Alps! Or take Ötzi the Ice Man, who died in the Italian Alps between 3350 and 3150 BCE. He suffered from parasites. His lungs were coated black from hut fires, damaged as badly as any modern-day cigarette smoker. Shortly before his death, he fought with three people, was wounded by an arrow, then fled and died in a sheltered gully. Some wild seeds caught in his clothing showed that he had climbed into the Alps from a village south of the mountains.

The Amesbury Archer and Ötzi provide intimate portraits of anonymous individuals. Now we can look over the shoulders of commoners and witness their hardships. The Egyptian pharaoh Akhenaten was, to put it mildly, a controversial ruler. After he came to the throne in 1349 BCE, he ordered the construction of his own capital including a magnificent temple to the sun god Aten, his favorite deity. He lived in great luxury with his queen, Nefertiti, but what was life like for the commoners who built his capital? Egyptologists excavated over 500 graves of Akhenaten's workers. The skeletons, from a cemetery of about 6,000 people, reveal chronic medical conditions resulting from hard labor—spinal trauma, fractured limbs, and arthritis, also widespread evidence of malaria and chronic dietary insufficiencies. Life was brutal and short.

Portraits of ancient societies will proliferate in future years. They will not make for a pretty sight, but they will give us a far more realistic appraisal of what life was really like in the past. They also make an important point. All of us are stakeholders in the human past, whether monarch, wealthy merchants, or anonymous slaves. For the first time, we are thinking about stakeholders. It's no coincidence that a great deal of today's archaeology now involves working with local communities, often tiny villages or native American settlements. World prehistory in a half century will be a far richer chronicle of human experience.

GENDER

For generations, the narrative of human prehistory was androcentric—male dominated, We tended to assume that all higher status activity such as hunting, toolmaking or creating art, was male work. Women were passive, weak, and private. Since the late 1960s, archaeologists have focused on gender identity, and how these identities were defined and realized in the past. Adding women to human prehistory has been a major step forward, a foundation for a new set of questions about the past.

Modern assumptions have long imbued archaeological thinking. Back in the 1880s, a Viking warrior was excavated at Bika, Sweden, lying with a long-bladed swords, a spear, and two sacrificed horses. For generations, the researchers assumed this was a man to be reckoned with. Then, in 2017, DNA proved that the skeleton was female. Viking sagas tell of shield maidens, who fought alongside male warriors. There must be other women warriors awaiting discovery.

Gender research is still at an early stage. Much depends on our mindsets, on our ability to look back at the past without bias. The feminist archaeologist Rosemary Joyce has reminded us that our position in society and history influences how we understand the past. Archaeologists must respect human dignity, including that of people unlike ourselves. This means that it is our responsibility to combat any form of inequality in the contemporary world. Thinking this way makes the past a powerful resource that archaeologists can draw upon with convincing authority.

So does world prehistory matter in today's industrialized world? It matters more than ever. We're achieving much improved understandings of ancient human behavior, and of our biological and cultural diversity that were unimaginable a few decades ago. We archaeologists are stewards of the magnificent cultural heritage of humanity, not only the Parthenon, or Maya Tikal, but also of the humble scatters of stone tools found on the fringes of the Sahara Desert. Our task is to present and preserve a past that we owe not only to ourselves and future generations but to those who created it. After all, we are all descended from the same African branch. We celebrate and preserve this reality, which is why world prehistory matters.

INDEX

Printed in the United States
by Baker & Taylor Publisher Services